THE
CHICANO
HERITAGE

This is a volume in the Arno Press collection

THE
CHICANO
HERITAGE

Advisory Editor
Carlos E. Cortés

Editorial Board
Rodolfo Acuña
Juan Gómez-Quiñones
George F. Rivera, Jr.

*See last pages of this volume
for a complete list of titles.*

The Mexican Aztec Society
A Mexican-American Voluntary Association
In Diachronic Perspective

Stanley A. West

ARNO PRESS

A New York Times Company

New York — 1976

Editorial Supervision: LESLIE PARR

———◆———

First publication in book form, 1976
  by Arno Press Inc.

Copyright © 1973 by Stanley A. West

THE CHICANO HERITAGE
ISBN for complete set: 0-405-09480-9
See last pages of this volume for titles.

Manufactured in the United States of America

———◆———

Library of Congress Cataloging in Publication Data

West, Stanley A
    The Mexican Aztec Society.

    (The Chicano heritage)
    Originally presented as the author's thesis,
Syracuse University.
    1. Mexican Americans--Pennsylvania--Bethlehem.
2. Bethlehem, Pa.--Social conditions. 3. Mexican
Aztec Society. I. Series.
F159.B5W47 1976   301.45'16'872074822   76-5230
ISBN 0-405-09532-5

THE MEXICAN AZTEC SOCIETY:

A MEXICAN-AMERICAN VOLUNTARY ASSOCIATION

IN DIACHRONIC PERSPECTIVE

by

STANLEY A. WEST

B. S., Syracuse University, 1965

ABSTRACT OF DISSERTATION

Submitted in partial fulfillment of the requirements for
the degree of Doctor of Philosophy in Anthropology
in the Graduate School of Syracuse University
May 1973

This dissertation describes the sole Mexican American voluntary association in Bethlehem, Pennsylvania. Analysis treats (1) the functions served by voluntary associations, (2) the accuracy of generalizations extant about changes which occur in voluntary associations, and (3) the nature of Mexican American associational behavior.

This work delineates services which the Mexican Aztec Society has rendered to members. Because changes within either the association's organization, goals, or operation all influence the members, these transformations are examined in detail. John Tsoudero's (1953) formalization model is employed for organization and analysis of the events transpiring within this association during its thirty-four years of existence. Lastly, this dissertation examines the notion that, because of their "maladaptive traditional culture," Mexican Americans can neither organize nor long maintain voluntary associations.

In accordance with Tsouderos's model, the Mexican Aztec Society has progressed from informal to increasingly formalized voluntary association: increased differentiation among membership statuses, growth in the membership body, attenuation of intragroup communication, decline of primary relationships, and eventually a general disaffection among members are observed. Throughout this association's history an expressive function has always been manifested. Also, to varying degrees participation (1) provides mutual assistance, (2) "cushions" the changes imposed upon new migrants by providing them with a "cultural bridge," (3) socializes members into novel modes of behavior, (4) permits members to either intensify or extend their social interactions, (5) provides members with opportunities for social or economic mobility, (6) serves as a source of intragroup unity. Through membership in the Mexican Aztec Society, Mexican Americans provide (1) a context for the dissemination of information, (2) preservation of Mexican American culture, (3) a framework for cultural pluralism, and (4) interaction with fellow ethnics.

As a manifest function members strive to foster social solidarity and a "love for work." As latent functions the association also provides for social control and communication among <u>colonias</u>. However, the fundamental associational function has always been symbolic: as a consequence of their participation members identify with Mexico and Mexican culture.

Moreover, because of historical accident, members achieved legal and social recognition of their association at approximately the same time that aspects of Latin culture became popular in the United States. At that time the Mexican Aztec Society rapidly expanded both its capital resources and its membership body; however in contrast with most other ethnic voluntary associations in Bethlehem, the association did not prosper as a result of support from <u>within</u> this ethnic group. As a consequence of the Mexican Aztec Society's departure from its fundamental function-- symbolic manifestation of identification with Mexico-- dependence upon the patronage of members not of Mexican descent has inevitably subjected this association to the vicissitudes of fadism and other forms of shifting popularity.

Mexican American voluntary associations are said to be hampered by members' tendency to participate **as if** the membership body constituted a primary group. However, in this case members' differing orientations toward fellow participants cause conflicts within the association: some members expect primary relationships to prevail while others expect secondary relationships. Nevertheless, members have, indeed, been able to provide the requisite leadership for the maintenance of their association. Furthermore, the Mexican Aztec Society manifests a rate of Mexican American participation which equals or surpasses the national average of association joining. In Bethlehem few Mexican Americans are poor, and, moreover, certain members successfully achieve social and economic mobility while preserving cultural pluralism. This research has yet to uncover any support for the belief that Mexican American culture is maladaptive or that Mexican Americans are unable to organize themselves.

THE MEXICAN AZTEC SOCIETY:

A MEXICAN-AMERICAN VOLUNTARY ASSOCIATION

IN DIACHRONIC PERSPECTIVE

by

STANLEY A. WEST

B. S., Syracuse University, 1965

DISSERTATION

Submitted in partial fulfillment of the requirements for
the degree of Doctor of Philosophy in Anthropology
in the Graduate School of Syracuse University
May 1973

PREFACE

This essay is based upon observations of a Mexican-American voluntary association in Bethlehem, Pennsylvania; fieldwork was conducted from December, 1969 through August, 1970. Due to the highly dispersed urban residential pattern of this group and also due to the advanced stage of the acculturation of this group, application of traditional anthropological research methods, such as participant observation, presented special problems. However, participant observation of the Mexican-Americans in the context of their sole formally organized group-wide voluntary association has proven profitable.

Moreover, this research leads to the conclusion that study of ethnic groups focused upon their voluntary association(s) constitutes an excellent opportunity for the observation of members of these groups as _ethnics_ rather than as blue collar workers, members of bowling leagues, church communicants, snowmobilers, or any other single locus of social behavior. In this sense the present research demonstrates that the study of urban voluntary associations permits anthropologists to maintain a traditional interest in discrete groups even when neighborhoods or communities may not provide feasible units for research.

As specific research problems this dissertation treats: (1) the functions served by voluntary associations, (2) the changes which occur within voluntary associations, and (3) the associational characteristics of Mexican Americans.

This dissertation could not have been prepared without assistance from many persons and institutions. The Ford Foundation, the Wenner-Gren Foundation for Anthropological Research and the University of Pennsylvania's Center for Urban Ethnography have supported either the research or the writing of this report, assistance which I gratefully acknowledge. This essay has profited from suggestions made by professors Agehananda Bharati, Gordon T. Bowles, D. Glynn Cochrane, Michael Freedman, John L. Gwaltney, and William Mangin who read the manuscript.

I wish to acknowledge the advice and editorial
assistance of Barbara W. Lex. Also, Irene Vasquez, Judy
Fonda, and Michael Howe have provided clerical assistance.

Of course, the Mexican Americans and other
residents of Bethlehem who almost without exception readily
cooperated with the investigation made this dissertation
possible. To the dozen or so informants who generously
contributed their time and insights far in excess of the
requirements of courtesy, I express my deep gratitude by
wishing that this work, indeed, accurately reflect their
perceptions of the Mexican Aztec Society rather than
solely the worldview of an anthropologist.

It should be noted that in order to respect the
privacy and confidentiality of informants' disclosures,
they are referred to by fictitious names throughout the
report.

TABLE OF CONTENTS

INTRODUCTION

Preliminary Remarks

This dissertation is about the sole voluntary
association of Mexican Americans in Bethlehem, Pennsylvania:
the Mexican Aztec Society.[1] During the course of participant observation of this association's many activities I
was able to examine a wide range of social interactions
among the members. Furthermore, having been granted access
to the association's records and having interviewed
participants, I have been able to make an analysis based
upon events in the association's thirty-four year history
which were recorded as they occurred by the members themselves. This two-pronged approach permits collection of
data which would have been unobtainable had I, like others,
exclusively depended upon social surveys for my information.

The General Problem

Despite several decades of anthropological study
of Mexican Americans, to date no descriptions of Mexican

[1]Voluntary associations are "institutionalized
groups in which membership is attained by joining (Little
1965: 1).

American voluntary associations are based upon systematic participant observation.[2] In particular, although questionnaires administered by Lane (1968), Officer (1964), and Barbosa-Dasilva (1968) do yield useful statistical information about leadership and membership participation, these researchers fail to make direct observation of associational activities. In order to initiate the accumulation of such accounts, this dissertation not only presents a diachronic description of one particular association but also tests the utility and validity of several analytical concepts and descriptive models which have been utilized heretofore in discussions of voluntary associations. Toward this end I present data and analysis which help to elucidate several questions. Briefly stated the questions treat the following topics (1) the functions served by voluntary associations, (2) the accuracy of generalizations made about changes which occur in associations, and (3) the nature of Mexican American associational behavior.

---

[2]Twenty years ago Julian Samora based his sociological dissertation (1953) upon participant observation of the voluntary associations in a southwestern Spanish American village; however he fails to describe any particular association in considerable detail (Watson & Samora 1954: 413-421). Nevertheless a doctoral study of Mexican American voluntary associations is now in preparation by Ann Rynearson of Washington University. As in the present research, Rynearson, too, relied primarily upon participant observation (Personal communication).

Functions Attributed to
Voluntary Associations

In the extensive literature which treats the
subject of voluntary associations various authors suggest,
based upon their own particular researches, a variety of
functions which voluntary associations purportedly serve
(Gordon and Babchuk 1959: passim; Warriner and Prather
1965:40; Hammond 1972: passim; Anderson 1971:213; Rose
1954:50; Hausknecht 1962:114-116; Banton 1956:358, 1957:
20-21, 193-195; Little 1965:47, 1971:12; Wallerstein 1964:
104; Frankenberg 1957: passim; Wheeldon 1969: passim;
Doughty 1970:154; Mangin 1965:318; Brandel-Srier 1971:46;
Noble 1970:203). In part, the number and diversity among
these alleged functions can be attributed to the dearth of
theory treating these social groups (Morris 1965:199).
Hence, a useful first step toward ultimate theorization is
to determine which of these many functions are observed in
empirical investigation. Moreover, researchers also imply
that a voluntary association serves the same single function
for most, if not all, of its members. In addition, most

accounts neglect changes in function because of a synchronic
emphasis. Accordingly, another purpose of this dissertation
is to delineate the functions which the Mexican Aztec
Society has served for various members and groups of
members throughout the thirty-four years of its existence.

Changes Within Voluntary Associations

With regard to the changes which occur within
voluntary associations, few investigators have hazarded
even a tentative working model of the general processes
which recur in associations. Nevertheless, from his study
of American voluntary associations, sociologist John
Tsouderos, concludes that associations manifest what he
terms the "formalization process." This he defines as
"the process by which groups follow prescribed patterns of
procedure; an increasing complexity in the social structure, a progressive prescription and standardization of
social relationships and finally, an increasing bureaucratization of the organization (Chapin and Tsouderos 1955:

306-309).[3] In other words, formalization includes the various processes which together account for the eventual transformation of informal voluntary associations into formal bureaucratic associations. Having never applied his scheme to any ethnic voluntary association, or to any association located beyond the boundaries of Minnesota, Tsouderos, nevertheless, claims a general applicability for his model. Because of the need for additional tests, I shall determine in this dissertation the degree to which his construct does account for empirical changes within the Mexican Aztec Society.[4]

Mexican American Associational Behavior

In discussions of the nature of Mexican American voluntary associations, one observes a marked inconsistency from one author to another despite a seemingly shared

---

[3] I credit Tsouderos rather than Chapin with this model because the notions were first published in Tsouderos's dissertation (1953:306). Statements made by anthropologist Immanuel Wallerstein about the evolution of African voluntary associations partially duplicate Tsouderos's model but Wallerstein's formulation neglects several aspects which Tsouderos elects to examine.

[4] Despite the need for a test of this model outside of the United States, to do so in Latin America, for example, would exceed the limits of this dissertation.

assumption that Mexican American culture is essentially homogeneous. Numerous authors assert, without unequivocable proof, that Mexican Americans cannot effectively organize themselves whether for expressive or for instrumental purposes (Rubel 1966:140-154; Macklin 1963:236-247; Lin 1963:92; Sargis 1966:173; Watson and Samora 1953:418; Grebler, Moore, and Guzman 1970:552; Alvarez 1971:69). The explanations employed result from an emphasis upon cultural determinism; that is, the cause of the purported inability to organize is said to lie in a "traditional culture" which is seen as both maladaptive and unchanging (Watson and Samora 1954:418; Lane 1968:4-5; Barbosa-Dasilva 1968:34; Grebler, Moore, and Guzman 1970:552; Sheldon 1966:127, 128, 145; Briegel 1970:128, 145, 161). However, other writers present evidence which leads to a contrary view, that Mexican Americans do manifest considerable organizational ability and, indeed, have formed many enduring voluntary associations (Officer 1964:26, 27, 29, 48, 53-56, 364, 365, 374; Lin 1963:92; Taylor 1934:173; Gonzales 1928:1; Arnold 1928:10; Taylor 1931a:63; 1932:131;

1934:173; Romano V. 1968:14-15; Grebler, Moore, and Guzman 1970:542-543; Galarza 1970:4; Lane 1968:53, 55, 183). In light of these discrepancies one not only concludes that further investigations are required but also that researchers should eschew a priori assumptions of homogeneous and maladaptive Mexican American culture as well as the correlative assumptions of organizational deficiencies among Mexican Americans. The foregoing assumptions demand proof, disproof, or further pertinent data.

Several more fundamental problems which arise in the description of Mexican American behavior and culture lie obscured behind these disagreements about Mexican American associations. Led by the anthropologist Actavio I. Romano - V, Mexican-American social scientists charge that major works written by sociologists and anthropologists distort Mexican American culture rather than provide accurate descriptions, and that frequent and uncritical reference to the concept of "traditional" Mexican American culture perpetuates stereotypes (Romano V. 1968:13-26; Alvarez 1971:68-77; Vaca 1971:17-51). Tuck, Kluckhohn,

Samora, Edmondson, Madson, Rubel, and others are said to
describe a static and homogeneous culture; furthermore
because of their belief in "traditional culture," these
non-Mexican Americans are seen to imply that throughout
their history Mexican Americans have been passive pawns,
rather than initiators of action. Hence, "traditional"
culture is identified as the impediment which prevents
Mexican Americans from creating organizations which in
turn can effect the group's social and economic mobility.
Indeed, Vaca accounts for the popularity of the concept of
traditional culture by suggesting that its use automatically
absolves all Anglo Americans from any responsibility for
Mexican American social problems; in other words, Mexican
Americans themselves are to blame for their predicament
because they chose to retain their maladaptive culture
(Vaca 1970:46).[5]

Many of these objects about descriptions of Mexican
Americans point to an over-zealous application of cultural
determinism on the part of the investigators. The possibility that these a priori assumptions of anthropologists,

[5]Anglo is a term which contrasts with Mexican
American but refers only to whites.

and others, have strongly biased their ethnographies indicates a need for anthropological researchers to remain open to causal factors which can supplant explanations couched solely in terms of traditional culture and cultural determinism. With this in mind I shall avoid cultural determinism in this work in order to test whether the criticisms which have been leveled at anthropologists can also stimulate development of viable alternatives.

Fieldwork

In December, 1969, I initiated field research among the Mexican Americans of Bethlehem, Pennsylvania. From that date through August, 1970, I applied a variety of investigation techniques but primarily I supplemented the technique of participant observation with use of open ended interviews. Although I did focus upon past and present members of the Mexican Aztec Society, I also interviewed many persons and examined various sources of data not directly related to this voluntary association.

Events Leading to Fieldwork

Choice of Bethlehem as a site for research largely depended upon my having fortuitously learned about the residence of Mexican Americans in Bethlehem. While visiting that city early in the fall of 1969, conversations about Mexico with two graduate students at Lehigh University, also in Bethlehem, elicited the information that there was a local population of "Mexicans." The students correctly informed me that the colonia had resulted from labor contracting by the Bethlehem Steel Corporation during the 1920's.[6] Intrigued by the notion of a small Mexican American enclave which had been isolated in the Northeast for nearly fifty years, I hastened to contact Mrs. Smith, who, according to the collegians, had investigated that ethnic group's local history. In a pattern that was to recur frequently during my later fieldwork, Mrs. Smith acknowledged little general familiarity with the colonia but, nevertheless, she named several of her Mexican-American acquaintances. The fragmentary information which I had obtained served only to pique my interest so

[6]La colonia mexicana, la colonia, or the colonia are all used to denote "the Mexican American population" of Bethlehem.

that after I left the Smith's home, I made a quick perusal of the grocery store listings in the yellow pages of the telephone book in an attempt to find the location of the "Mexican neighborhood." Indeed, a few Spanish-named groceries did exist, but several hours of driving around Bethlehem's south side and conversations with proprietors turned up no Mexican Americans, but a great number of Puerto Ricans! The Spanish-named businesses were neither owned nor patronized by the elusive Mexican Americans; nor did any of these particular persons know the location of Mexican Americans. At that point in time I first began to doubt the existence of a geographically distinct <u>colonia mexicana</u>.

Attempts to establish contact with the Mexican Americans whose names Mrs. Smith had provided did not prove immediately successful: in the first case after explaining my academic interest in the history of the Mexican Americans of Bethlehem, a man who I telephoned replied that "I don't have much to do with Mexicans." In the second case, a woman also demurred, but at the same

time volunteered that "my mother [then visiting Mexico]
or Sr. Tejeda are the people for you to see." Not wishing
to chance the impersonality of another telephone call, I
followed her suggestion that I seek Mr. Rejeda at the
Mexican Aztec Society's quarters. After finding the
clubhouse of this voluntary association, I diffidently
asked (in Spanish) for Sr. Tejeda. The "old timer" had
some difficulty grasping the notion of a study of Mexican
Americans in Bethlehem, but president Frank Sanchez quickly
comprehended the notion and assisted me in presenting the
explanation. As soon as Sr. Tejeda understood my research
interest, however, he readily provided me with further
information about his colonia. Sr. Tejeda also volunteered
to sponsor me for social membership in the association as
well as offering me the hospitality of a "drink on the
house." At our conversation's close, Sr. Tejeda encouraged
me to return to "the club" in the near future.[7] Also, he

---

[7]I employ the following as synonyms: Mexican Aztec
Society, Sociedad Azteca Mexicana, Mexican Association, and
when the context is clear, "the association." Also, the
term "Aztecan" denotes "member of the Mexican Aztec Society."
However. "the club" or "the Mexican club" denotes the
Mexican Aztec Society's clubhouse and the activities which
regularly occur within it; this usage is employed by the
members themselves.

accepted my offer of a ride to his home. Perhaps mention
of three summers spent in Mexico as well as the fact that
I conversed in Spanish partly accounts for the receptivity
of both Sanchez and Tejeda. Needless to say, I felt
encouraged by this first direct contact with Mexican
Americans.

Because I had discovered that activities at the
club ordinarily take place at night, I spent the next day
at local libraries (vide 7 supra). Examination of card
catalogs in addition to conversations with several
librarians persuaded me that I would not find written
descriptions of the area's Mexican Americans. In another
fortuitous encounter, Thomas Vadasz, who was engaged in
research in the library at the same time, overheard this
conversation. After introducing himself as a graduate
student investigating the topic of immigrant history in
Bethlehem, he provided several source materials which have
been most useful to the present research and also suggested
the names of several Lehigh University faculty who proved
to be helpful (Vadasz 1967; n.d.).

Thus armed with written as well as oral data about Bethlehem's Mexican Americans, I composed the proposal for the present study which was then accepted by my doctoral committee. Although I had not as yet been funded for the investigation, I obtained a loan which enabled me to relocate to Bethlehem in December, 1969. Immediately I began fieldwork. In view of the absence of any geographic concentration of Mexican American residences, research considerations did not dictate that I live in any particular area of this city.

Contact

As soon as I had "moved in," I sought Sr. Tejeda at the Mexican Aztec Society's clubhouse. To my surprise I found that about thirty Mexican Americans had already contregated there that evening in anticipation of a regular monthly business meeting. Sr. Tejeda and Frank Sanchez recognized me and promptly introduced me to individual members of the "assembly" seated along the bar--including one woman who had been contacted initially--and explained the purpose of the study. Sr. Tejeda also sponsored me for

membership in the association.[8] No objections ensuing, I
then observed the business meeting and informally interviewed several members afterward. While departing from
the building, one "old timer" extended an invitation to
talk further at his home. As I later discovered, the
mexican Americans both respect Sr. Tejeda and also view
him as a "pillar of the community." Despite his somewhat
inaccurate description of my research aims, introductions
by Sr. Tejeda did facilitate my acceptance by other Mexican
Americans.

After the first evening's fieldwork I concluded
that Sr. Tejeda had been correct in recommending "the
Mexican club" as a "good place to meet Mexicans"; membership in the voluntary association also promised to provide
a convenient context for observation of Mexican Americans.

Revision of Research Design

According to my original design I had planned to
apply the mathematics of graph theory in order to investigate the relationship of Mexican American social networks
to further aspects of their group's social organization

[8]Members of the Mexican Aztec Society are referring
to "voting members who attend a business meeting" whenever
they use the term "assembly."

(Harary and Norman 1953). However, a preliminary elicita-
tion of social networks demonstrated that non-Mexican
Americans constitute the majority of Mexican Americans'
social contacts. To have arbitrarily restricted the network
links to Mexican Americans would have severely biased the
network data, and to have processed data concerning far
more non-Mexican Americans than Mexican Americans would
have transformed the research into a study of Bethlehem,
Pennsylvania, rather than an investigation of one ethnic
group.[9] Although I then abandoned my prior plans to focus
upon social networks, I did observe that Mexican Americans'
social networks are most likely to intersect for Mexican
Americans who are either kinsmen or fellow members of the
Mexican Aztec Society.[10] In the absence of a viable
strategy for detailed observation of kinsmen who might
reside throughout some twenty or more square miles, I
elected to base much of my study upon those Mexican

---

[9]Anthropologist J.A. Barnes also lends support to
this decision by cogently criticizing the application of
graph theory to the analysis of social networks (1972:5-6).
    I shall define ethnic groups as "categories of
ascription and identification by the actors themselves, and
thus have the characteristic of organizing interaction
between people" (Barth 1969:10).
    [10]In his study of Nova Scotian Negroes, Whitten
(1970:389) indicated that for this group church provided
the sole context of symbolic expression.

Americans who associate together as members of the Mexican
Aztec Society.

Status and Role

In my study of the Mexican Aztec Society I participated in the association's formal status of "social
member." Although non-members can enter the clubhouse in
the company of a member, such persons in the status of
"guest" are legally barred the purchase, but not consumption, of alcoholic beverages. Social membership guarantees
entry to the clubrooms any night of the week as well as
purchase of alcoholic beverages on the premises; it does
not, however, entitle a vote in association matters or the
receipt of benefits for sickness or death. The latter
rights accord only to Mexican Americans and their spouses
who pay the more costly dues which are required of "active
members." Social membership, for which I did qualify,
satisfied my research needs in that this role permitted me
sustained contact with association members.

Whenever I met a Mexican American I found some way
in which to describe my status of researcher. I explained

that I was endeavoring to learn about the entire history of
the Mexican Americans of Bethlehem, including events of
the most recent years. This explanation of purpose, along
with knowledge of Spanish and earlier travels in Mexico,
may have seemed unusual to a few Mexican Americans who
may never have decided how to classify me.[11]

During several weeks of visiting the clubhouse
every evening, I developed excellent rapport with the
association's officers as well as with those of the members
who served as volunteer workers. One Saturday night when
few members were in evidence, the steward approached me
with an unusual request, asking, "Hey, will you go 'card'
people at the door?" Beginning with that evening I served

---

[11]For example, despite repeated protestations to
the contrary, informants invariably identified me to
others as a student at Lehigh University, the only university in the Bethlehem area; most members could not
grasp the notion of a student leaving his university in
order to engage in research. In passing, however, it
might be noted that such persistent misidentification
testifies to the considerable impact of Lehigh University
upon Bethlehem, particularly with respect to its location
on the "south side"--a traditional residential district
for immigrant groups in that city.

as doorman, or some other quasi-official status in the
association, approximately once each week throughout the
remainder of the field experience.[12]

Frequently while I was on duty, one of the officers
would join me in conversation at the door; thus, an opportunity for participant observation, as well as a visible
and legitimate status in the activities of the voluntary
association, was provided. Although service as doorman
provided me with opportunity to meet and interact with
Mexican Americans, nevertheless these encounters were
generally rather brief. Hence, one Saturday evening
when the steward could find no other bartender, I found
myself colunteered. In this new capacity I was able to

----

[12]In this context, "carding" refers to the checking
of patrons' membership cards as required by the Pennsylvania
Liquor Control Board. The person stationed at the club's
entrance may only admit active and social members and their
guests (these persons must be over twenty-one years of age).
Furthermore, the doorman collects membership dues of $2.00
per year from current social members or from persons who
are applying for membership. (Active members are assessed
$1.00 per month, which they pay directly to either the
treasurer or the financial secretary.) Also, the doorman
oversees the signing of the "guest book" in keeping with
a regulation of the Pennsylvania State Liquor Control
Board. In the past members received a salary of $2.00
per hour for the performance of these services; at present,
however, members working at the door are compensated only
with "a few drinks on the house."

meet and observe the many Mexican Americans who rarely enter the clubhouse except when they come there for recreation purposes on Saturday nights--the only time when the featured entertainment is Latin American dance music. Furthermore, as a direct consequence of my status as bartender, I became acquainted with several key informants.[13]

Because of informants' sex roles, investigators who have studied Mexican-Americans invariably admit to possessing relatively complete data for only half of the subject population: the half which is of the same sex as themselves. In part, this phenomenon results from the reluctance of Mexican-American informants to interact with researchers of the opposite sex. Furthermore, anthropologists have explained this phenomenon by discussing traditional Mexican American culture: it is an expectation that women are

---

[13]Herbert Gans (1962:388-389) identifies three types of participant observation approaches: researcher acts as observer, in which case the researcher is present but his main function is to observe, refraining from affecting the phenomenon being studied as much as can be avoided; researcher participates, but as researcher, in which case the researcher becomes an actual participant only in terms of his research interests; and researcher participates, an approach in which the observer role is temporarily abdicated. Participant observation in the study reported herein has included these three variations in approach. However, of the three types, the second was the most difficult to effect while on the premises of the club.

sheltered and protected from contacts with males, male anthropologists notwithstanding. In contrast, female anthropologists generally cannot frequent the bars and pool rooms in which many male Mexican Americans pass their leisure time; therefore the context of female anthropologists' participant observation is limited to the home and interactions confined to children and adult women. Hence, the sex of the fieldworker generally biases any description of Mexican-American life (Rubel 1962:31; Macklin 1963: 10; Matthiasson 1968:31).

The Mexican Americans of Bethlehem are slightly more receptive to the idea of investigators who interact with informants of both sexes than are some other groups of Mexican Americans; nevertheless in this research contacts with males were decidedly more frequent than were contacts with females. To some extent the imbalance results from male interference: to illustrate, on one occasion I asked a male informant the name of a woman in her late forties. forties. The informant ignored the question; instead he grunted, "She's married." Moreover, in the course of visiting the homes of some first generation Mexican Americans, the wives immediately departed from the room leaving their husbands alone with the researcher. Yet, on the few occasions when the wife did remain, even if it appeared that she might have proved a more useful informant than her husband, as shown by her expressed knowledge as well as by her interest in the reason for the visit, I felt that I would have failed to show proper respect to the elderly man if I were to have concentrated my attention upon interviewing the wife.

Nevertheless, although the Mexican Americans of Bethlehem do exhibit attitudes which impede cross-sex participant observation, far greater importance should be attached to the observation that females spend much less time at the association's clubhouse than do males. Because I focused my research up on the voluntary association, I interacted more with males than with females. However, as aides in the compilation of the colonia census, female Mexican Americans contributed their time more generously than did males. Given the patterns of defacto sexual

segregation which exist among Azteca members, I necessarily
devote slightly greater attention to males than to females.

To Mexican Aztec Society members I was not merely
friend, student, researcher, social member, doorman and
bartender. Although only approximately two years the
junior of two association officers, I sometime perceived
that they had fondly adopted me as "kid" although not once
did they utter this term. In this case my status as
student and my lack of employment may have stimulated
informants to treat me as a rather young adult. Nevertheless, many members expressed respect for my university
education and on more than one occasion I found myself in
the potentially dangerous position of being asked to settle
a dispute on the basis of my factual knowledge.

Routine of Fieldwork

Although my daily schedule almost without fail
included an evening visit to the bar of the Mexican Aztec
Society, the research design included daytime interviewing
of retired Mexican Americans or certain local non-Mexican
Americans. The non-Mexican Americans whom I contacted

include businessmen, government officials, clergymen, labor
union officers, executives of the Bethlehem Steel Corporation, and medical doctors who have interacted with members
of the colonia mexicana.

From such interviews I learned about attitudes
toward this ethic group.[14] In some instances this information contrasted either with the Mexican Americans' self
images or with my observations of the colonia. For example,
some Bethlehem residents go so far as to categorically deny
their existence, insisting that "there aren't any Mexicans
here at all anymore--they all went back home." Also, a
number of older non-Mexican Americans describe members of
the colonia as having been hot-tempered and prone to
knife-fighting; in contrast, Mexican Americans picture
themselves merely as having been poor but hard working
laborers.

In many interviews the local people also named
particular Mexican Americans known to them whom, they felt,
I should interview. In point of fact, however, many of the
Mexican Americans so named were persons who, at least at

[14]The importance of such attitudes to research on
urban groups has been elaborated on in a working paper, in
collaboration with my wife, produced during the study (Lex
and West 1970).

the present time, appear to play no active role either in
the Azteca or in the colonia.

At least once each day, usually at night, I
dictated my observations into a portable tape recorder.
In order to avoid possible inhibition on the part of
informants, as well as prohitively large numbers of
recorded tapes, I depended upon memory and, at times,
brief observations written in a pocket notebook. Moreover,
I confined my note taking to times when I surmised that
the informant would not be made ill at ease. Furthermore,
based upon his reaction to brief jottings of information, I
decided whether I could also take detailed notes. While on
the premises of the Mexican Aztec Society, a discreet visit
to the privacy of the toilet sometimes facilitated the
recording of especially detailed information. However, I
discovered that the most effective procedure on days when
I had scheduled several different interviews was to carry
the tape recorder in the car and to record a detailed
description of each session immediately thereafter. In
this study use of a tape recorder permitted the collection

of greater amounts of data than could otherwise have been
obtained during the eight-some months which were available
for fieldwork.

In order to observe the interactions of Mexican
Americans who only participate in formal, organizational
activities, I always endeavored to be present during the
regular monthly meetings of the association. Usually I
seated myself among members of the "assembly" ("active"
members attending the meeting). At no time did anyone
express objection to my presence, although in point of
fact social members are permitted no voice in association
matters and the by-laws neither guarantee nor deny to
social members the right to attend such business meetings.

Developments During Fieldwork

Despite my growing realization that the Mexican
Aztec Society provided the best single focus for my
research, I did continue to seek out data about the entire
colonia. To illustrate, one evening while bartending at
the clubhouse, I explained my research project to two
middle-aged Mexican American women. After describing the

frustrations of attempting to learn about a group which is residentially so dispersed, I exclaimed, "why, I don't know who all the Mexicans are or even how many there are!" In response to the woman's reply that "you know, we don't either," I suggested that if they so desired, the woman could compile the names of many Mexican Americans from memory and that such a census would be very useful to the study. After expressing personal interest in the compilation of such data, both women then volunteered to enlist other kinsmen in the preparation of a census.

Because these informants chose their own ordering principles in their first draft of the Mexican American census, the structure and content of that data set reflect the cognitive orientation of the informants rather than that of the investigator. To illustrate, the informants initially listed conjugal unions in which one or both spouses were elderly first generation Mexican Americans. They next recorded the names of unmarried first generation Mexican Americans. Variants include persons who "married late in life" or who "never married." In the case of any

Mexican American who had a spouse not of recent immigrant stock, these women chose to parenthetically denote the spouse as "American." Discounting names of persons who had either moved to Mexico after retirement or died, these informants listed the names of seventy-four first generation Mexican Americans and indicated numbers rather than names of offspring.

By no means did a lack of dedication on the part of my volunteer informants cause them to restrict their compilation to "old timers." Rather, confusion arose in the use of ethic labels. I had learned early in my field-work that few Mexican Americans of Bethlehem admit any ethnic term except "Mexican." In this dissertation I do employ "Mexican American" because of its greater descrip-tive value, but in Bethlehem I became accustomed to using the locally accepted category of "Mexican." What the first census demonstrated was that informants attach at least three meanings to "Mexican": (1) Mexican-born founder of the colonia, (2) any Mexican-born person, (3) person of Mexican origin or descent. Although I had intended the third definition of this ambiguous term, my informants chose the first. Henceforth, because of such problems of semantics, I had to speak of "Mexicans and persons of Mexican descent" in order to avoid any unintentional exclusion of local Mexican Americans.

As a second stage I remedied the situation by providing the informants with mimeographed census sheets for each conjugal union which elicited such information as age, birthplace, education, names of children, and other data. In completing the census forms the women compiled data in order of descent from the colonia's founders. Third and finally, I compiled a master list of persons of possible Mexican descent who were either named by the women, appeared in high school graduation lists, or mentioned in association records. These several informants then deleted from the master list any names of Puerto Rican, Spanish, or Portuguese persons, thus producing a fairly accurate census.

Considering the fact that few Mexican Americans today know all other Mexican Americans, the census must be

taken as an approximation, but also as the best available
estimate: approximately seven hundred Mexican Americans
reside in Bethlehem, a city of about 80,000.[15]

After providing me with a copy of the first census,
Constance Estrada had invited me to her home so that I
might explain my additional data needs to a group composed
of herself, her sisters, sisters-in-law, and mother. In
my research I have adopted the policy of visiting informants
in the company of my wife only when the event promised to
become rather social in character, but on this particular
occasion it soon became obvious that the Mexican American
women were not at all reticent in the presence of a strange
couple although they might have been less open in the
presence of one male researcher. The discussion touched
upon many topics not directly related to the census, such
as birth control and abortion, which might not otherwise
have been discussed. As a further outcome, without prompting
Constance Estrada invited me, along with my spouse, to be

---

[15]The 1970 Census of Population which counts only
first and second generation Mexican American estimates the
size of the colonia mexicana at five hundred and forty-eight
(Table 81). Without doubt, when third generation residents
are included, at least seven hundred Mexican Americans
reside in Bethlehem.

guests at the Fourth of July picnic traditionally attended by her extended family.

The willingness of the Mexican American women to prepare a census of their colonia proved to be essential for general knowledge about local Mexican Americans because attempts to administer questionnaires proved impossibly difficult by virtue of the prevalence of the "swing shift" among blue collar steelworkers. Because the time of an employee's shift varies from day to day according to a complex cycle, if I were to visit three informants at approximately 2:00 p.m. on a Tuesday, one might be asleep, another might be at work, and another might be visiting the Jersey shore during his four day "weekend."

The fluidity of the working hours of steelworkers not only makes it difficult for an interviewer to encounter informants at home--unless by careful pre-arrangement--it also precludes the likelihood that both the husband and the working wife will be at home simultaneously. Only by making many return visits could I complete a mere twenty interview forms. In order to maximize the all-too-brief time in the field, I elected to concentrate upon participant observation in the club rather than devote precious time to formal interviewing.

About six weeks in advance of May 5, the occasion of an important annual ceremonial at the association's clubhouse, one of the officers approached me with the falttering request that I present the "key note address" on the history of the <u>colonia</u> as part of the oratory following the banquet. Not only apprehensive about speaking before such a large number of people, but also undecided about the mechanics of developing a speech appropriate in both level and content, I vacillated. After I eventually declined, the officers added yet another politician to the speaker's roster, a move which turned out to be in consonance with the general themes of the speeches, and which also perhaps revealed one of the latent functions of such ceremonial occasions for ethnically-based voluntary associations in Bethlehem: such events provide contexts for local political activity.

Observation of this special event also brought into
high relief the sexual segregation which characterized many
of the "ordinary" activities of the Mexican Aztec Society.
In contrast, the Cinco de Mayo celebration was decidedly
a "couples" affair (as are evenings at the clubrooms when
there is 'live' entertainment) but on weekday nights men
predominate at the clubhouse bar. Although women and men
participate in the association's regular monthly meetings
and some women have served as recording secretary, there
is also a functioning Ladies Auxiliary in which membership
is limited to the female sex.

Through the fieldwork I endeavored to obtain as
much data as possible on the history of the Mexican Aztec
Society and its members. In the final month of my research,
association officers granted me access to the organization's
minutes of meetings, correspondence files, and membership
lists. Because the minutes had been recorded only in
Spanish for nearly twenty years following the association's
formation in 1937, it was necessary to hire translation
services in order to obtain English copies in a minimum

amount of time; however to verify the accuracy of the
Cuban translators, residents of nearby Allentown, I spot-
checked sample pages.[16] With some confidence I can state
that the translations of the minutes are faithful render-
ings of the original texts. Because the limited time
which remained for field research precluded me from
interviewing all present or past members of the association
in order to verify, clarify, or amplify the written
descriptions, this study is truncated in that regard.
Generation of participation indices for members mentioned
one or more times in the minutes also permitted me to
identify members of the voluntary association whose high
degree of involvement required further investigation. For
the purpose of discovering temporal patterns associated
with the Mexican Aztec Society, I made a detailed content
analysis of all association minutes (Holsti 1969). These
data usefully complement the nonanalytical recollections of

---

[16]Although several Cubans belong to the Mexican
Aztec Society as social members and patronize the bar on
Saturday nights, these few Cubans live outside of
Bethlehem. Because they feel that they are of a higher
social status, Cubans say that they "do not mix socially"
with the Mexican Americans. Indeed, the translators were
somewhat amused by the "quaint" grammar and spelling to be
found in the Mexican Aztec Society's minutes.

elderly informants who often confuse either details or chronology. Some secretaries incorporated many details into their minutes, others included little information. Indeed, for the association's protection some illegal events were completely omitted. Therefore, I had to evaluate the accuracy of each item without the benefit of a complete transcription of each meeting's transactions. Nevertheless, despite variation in the thoroughness and preciseness with which meetings were described, the minutes of the Mexican Aztec Society do afford the best single source of diachronic information about this association.

It is the purpose of this dissertation to apply observations and analyses about the Mexican Aztec Society to several general questions: (1) the functions served by voluntary associations, and (2) the accuracy of generalizations made about changes which occur in voluntary associations, and (3) the nature of Mexican American associational behavior. I begin with an expanded statement of the problem followed by a description of the setting in which the Mexican Aztec Society was organized. This milieu encompasses the city of Bethlehem where the Mexican immigrants settled; particular attention is devoted to the colonia mexicana which they founded in 1923. I then focus upon the Mexican Aztec Society while placing primary emphasis upon several temporal processes which can be identified in the period from 1937 to 1970. In order to treat the contemporary functions of this voluntary association I then describe and analyze the interactions among members whom I observed in 1970. I conclude with a summary of the empirical data and an analysis of the heuristic frameworks which have been tested for the case of the Mexican Aztec Society.

CHAPTER I

THE PROBLEM

Preliminary Remarks

Having briefly introduced the problem to which this dissertation is addressed, the present chapter presents this problem in considerable amplification. To begin, associational functions of varying generality are described in order to identify working hypotheses which lend themselves, as heuristics, to examination of functions of the Mexican Aztec Society of Bethlehem, Pennsylvania. Despite its brevity, the discussion of the formalization process of voluntary associations which follows should not be taken as belittlement of its contribution to this dissertation. Lastly, developments in the study of Mexican American culture, as well, are treated in detail in order to fully establish the relationship of this dissertation to anthropological knowledge about Mexican American associational behavior.

Associational Functions

Social scientists who investigate voluntary associations ascribe to them a multiplicity of functions. As a consequence of the fact that many anthropologists have studied ethnic voluntary associations, rather than other types of associations which are both numerous and diverse, I shall most thoroughly treat the functions provided by ethnic organizations. However, in order to impose some order upon the numerous descriptions of voluntary associations, the functions of these organizations shall be grouped according to the populations which most benefit from associational activities: social groups, or individual members. Because social groups of maximal size constitute entire societies, discussion of the services which associations render for groups of persons pertains to societies, part-societies such as ethnic populations, and even small aggregates of individuals.

Group Functions of Voluntary Associations

At the societal level voluntary associations are
credited with several accomplishments. First, they foster
societal integration by creating channels of communication
among groups of individuals (including governmental bodies)
and by crosscutting many kinship or territorial groups.[1]
Secondly, they contribute to necessary processes of
societies including "decision-making, opinion formation,
and socialization" (Babchuk and Warriner 1965:135). Thirdly,
numerous American social scientists, especially sociologist
Arnold M. Rose, extoll the virtues of the voluntary association as an institution which supports political democracies.
In his discussion Rose contends that associations give
many citizens a share of political power. Moreover, by
permitting or encouraging many persons to participate in
activities which may even eventually affect the course of
their entire society, associations augment individuals'
satisfactions with democratic process (Rose 1954:50;
Hausknecht 1962:114-116).

[1]Sociologists frequently term this notion "the
integration hypothesis" (Babchuk and Edwards 1965:149;
Sills 1968:374).

However, Bernard Barber (1956:485-486) calculates that in even the most activist of associations no more than five to seven percent of the members participate actively and not even required presence at meetings results in token attendance. By no means can it be said that joining a voluntary association automatically inspires persons to contribute to democratic processes whether in an association or in politics. As demonstrated by this and other associational participation studies, Rose overstates his case even for large-scale modern states with a democratic political structure. Associations' functions which deal with social integration, decision-making, opinion formation, and socialization potentially apply to all societies; however the function, support for political democracy, necessitates the prior existence of this particular political process.

In Rose's view voluntary associations may also serve as "instruments of social change" (op. cit.). Without doubt, some voluntary associations do indeed impel social change within entire societies. In the United States many governmental functions which were once provided

by voluntary associations, such as formal education, payment for medical care, and unemployment insurance, have
become governmental responsibilities because of the
political influence of voluntary associations. To cite
another example, in Africa's Gold Coast voluntary associations sponsored literacy programs long before the national
government adopted the idea and embarked upon a mass
education program (Wallerstein 1964:104). Based upon
considerations from organization theory, sociologist David
Sills (1959:21) concludes that the utility of voluntary
associations as instruments of social change is inherently
limited by the fact that associations are also simultaneously objects of change. Frequently members find themselves
deflected from their original goals as a consequence of
measures taken merely for the purpose of maintaining the
organization's day-to-day existence. Because the activities
of associations formed for the purpose of fomenting a
social change will achieve or always seek precisely that
same goal.

To continue this discussion of voluntary associations as instruments of change, one observes that Michael Banton's research further illuminates the problem (1957:163-83). He establishes that, at least in some cases, the members of an entire African tribe can elevate their group's social status by means of associational activity. Despite their "modern" orientation, Temne migrants to Freetown found themselves relegated to a low social status. Furthermore, because of lack of formal education this avenue of upward social mobility was closed to most of them. In response to this situation the Temne organized voluntary associations called dancing compins (companies) in order to demonstrate their "progressiveness." The recreation provided by these associations soon stimulated persons from several other tribes to seek membership in Temne compins and, as a result, the social status of the Temne began to climb. The greatest augmentation in tribal prestige came after the Temne association members successfully mobilized themselves in order to elect a young educated Temne to the post of Tribal Headman. The new Headman, who had also organized the first

<u>compin</u>, was able to extend the authority of his post because of support from members of dancing companies. With the political backing of these "modernists" the Headman counteracted the power of the conservative elders and so energized the Temne Tribal Administration that other tribes began to admire the Temne both in their homeland and in the city. Although the evidence leads to the conclusion that voluntary associations can potentially cause social change at the societal level, the efficacy of these organizations for this purpose cannot be guaranteed. However, a more thorough treatment of the societal functions of voluntary associations would exceed the scope of this dissertation.

In order to facilitate analysis of voluntary associations, several American sociologists have devised typologies which apply both to group functions and also to individual functions. The scheme which has been most widely adopted, that of Gordon and Babchuck (1959: <u>passim</u>), consists of two polar types complemented by a intermediate type of mixed characteristics. First, "expressive"

associations are those which maximize the satisfactions
felt by the members while in the course of performing
their membership roles. Second, "instrumental" associations
are those which concentrate upon the production of goods
or services, the achievement of some change in a society,
or other group goals whether latent or manifest. Third,
associations which encompass both of the foregoing are
identified as "instrumental-expressive." In the order
presented these three associational types underscore
individual functions, group functions, and a combination
of the two. Despite wide applicability of this framework,
one may question its utility because only gross distinctions
are made among the types. In making yet finer discrimina-
tions among several functions of voluntary associations,
Warriner and Prather focus upon the rewards of individuals.
To these authors, associations (1) provide "pleasure in
the performance" of the membership role ("pleasure" function),
(2) foster the communication toward which members already
incline ("sociability" function), (3) reinforce a prized
belief system ("symbolic" function), or (4) realize some

goal ("productive" function) (1965:5). Because of the near
equivalence in the usage of the terms pleasure and expressive as well as productive and instrumental, I shall herein
adopt "instrumental" and "expressive" in light of their
wider acceptance by anthropologists. If one notes that
particular voluntary associations manifest various functions
to varying degrees, one need not single out instrumental-
expressive as a single function. Therefore, the functions
of voluntary associations which remain are expressive,
instrumental, sociability, and symbolic.

As organizations created for the furtherance of
shared special interests, many voluntary associations
function for the benefit of particular groups of persons.
The International Red Cross provides care for victims of
war and other disasters; participants in a Mesoamerican
cargo system serve their community by organizing religious
celebrations (Carrasco 1961); Brazilian businessmen who
join a panelinha (always informal and secret) profit as a
group, because each member guarantees preferential economic
relationships with the others (Leeds 1965:393-398). As

these illustrations of particular groups indicate, functions of instrumental voluntary associations may either pertain the group of members or to some group of non-members.

The published description of voluntary associations make it clear that these organizations manifest highly diverse instrumental group functions. As illustration of this point, one observes that in addition to modifying their town milieu, members of various African associations also induce change within their tribal areas. In Lagos, Nigeria, members of one regional association compelled their village elders to reduce the amount of brideprice. The youths had made the strategic threat not to marry any girl from their villages until the time when the brideprice might be lowered (Comhaire 1950:234-236). But to members of a rural Tanzanian population, the Basukuma, the existence of voluntary associations in the villages gives the villagers a means of relating to outside influences. There the Catholic church has been "assigned the status of voluntary association . . . and related to accordingly" (Hamer 1967: 199). Moreover, because of their perceived inability to

"come together in informal association and friendly home
entertainment, the African elites of Reeftown, South Africa
continue their support of voluntary associations which
regularly organize "social events" (Brandel-Srier 1971:52).
In each of these instances the associations have instrumental group functions; however for the Reeftown elite the
instrumental function of their associations is to provide
for sociability among members.

In their discussions of conflicts within voluntary
associations, several researchers, notably Frankenberg and
Wheeldon, identify a possible latent function in the
conflict which can exist within associations; conflict can
directly contribute to group social integration (North
et al.,1960; Frankenberg 1957; Wheeldon 1969). According
to Wheeldon, in South Africa both Whites and Coloreds
subscribe to the belief that Coloureds cannot avoid constant strife in their associations. But in each conflict
several types of recurring sanctions compel the members of
competing interest groups to uncover some source of unity.
Because the Coloureds have few prestigious voluntary

associations in which they can attain prominence, socially
ambitious Coloureds belong to several and must also preserve a public image of cooperation with fellow-officers;
past antagonists are compelled to work together within
various organizations. However, this image of cooperation
is not mere fiction. Once a conflict erupts members of
the antagonists's social networks exert intense pressure
on them to find a basis for conflict resolution and subsequent cooperation. Coloureds feel that at any cost they
must avoid reinforcing the belief that their organizations
are rife with conflict. Furthermore, antagonistic Coloured
officers _must_ resolve their conflicts, at least publicly,
because otherwise they would never again be elected to an
associational office. This recurrent process of conflict
and resolution also has the effect of encouraging recon-
sideration of accepted values and norms (_Ibid._:179). On
the one hand, Wheeldon suggests that social integration is
supported _despite_ the frequent conflicts among association
members while, on the other hand, he suggests that conflicts
stimulate adjustments in cultural expectations in the

direction of greater appropriateness for the present
milieu. In either case he establishes that conflict among
members of voluntary associations may serve one or more
latent instrumental functions.

Frankenberg's description of Pentre, a Welsh
village, leads to the conclusion that at least in this
instance interpersonal conflict is necessary for the
preservation of village unity if not for the preservation
of Pentre as a community (rather than as a mere aggregate
of residences). Frankenberg also implies that without
local voluntary associations there would be little cooperative activity in the village. During the past several
years "Pentre people" have always had at least one voluntary
association at any particular time: "Village choir, brass
band, dramatic society, football club, carnival" (3-4).
Frankenberg suggests that it is the symbolic function of
each association that is of supreme importance. Each
association represents Pentre's existence as a community.
However, because of the conflicts which inevitably erupt
and eventually polarize the entire population, no

association remains viable for more than a few years.
Here, as in South Africa, villagers do not tolerate open
conflict or, expressed differently, whenever a schism
reaches the extent that it bursts into the open, the
association has already been doomed. In yet another sense
the image of Pentre unity is achieved by making "outsiders"
committee chairmen. However, rather than being permitted
to lead, these outsiders are actually led by the villagers
by way of informal pressures. But above all these "strangers"
spare Pentre people from an "irremediable breach of
relationship" (Ibid). In Pentre, outsiders, like Whites
in South Africa, serve as the scape goats said to destroy
local unity. Although leaders as well as associations are
expended, Pentre residents, nevertheless, successfully
preserve their existence as a community. Hence, the
symbolic function of voluntary associations in Pentre
eclipses any instrumental functions which the associations
may also provide.

Recognition of expressive, instrumental, sociability, and symbolic aspects of voluntary associations

contributes to analyses of the group functions of these organizations. Furthermore, this typology of functions also contributes to the elucidation of associational functions viz-a-viz the members as individuals.

Each of the associational functions which this section are described in were derived from empirical investigations within at least one area of the world. However, those group functions which are particular to Mexican American voluntary associations must be established through direct observation. Without citing his evidence one Mexican American, Salvador Alvarez, claims that members of Mexican American voluntary associations recognize four functions of their organizations (1971:75): to provide for (1) "the preservation of the general Mexican-American way of life" (instrumental and symbolic), (2) a variety of organizations to join (instrumental), (3) "informational and communication networks" (instrumental and sociability), and (4) a framework of cultural pluralism (instrumental). Because Alvarez does not present detailed empirical evidence in support of his hypothesized functions, I shall test

their applicability to the colonia mexicana of Bethlehem,
Pennsylvania.

An instrumental and sociability function not
admitted by Alvarez also appears applicable to Mexican
American associations in Bethlehem. In her analysis of
Greek American voluntary associations in Boston, Mary
Treudley establishes that these organizations have the
effect of "maintaining interaction among Greek Americans"
(1966:60). Like the Mexican Americans of Bethlehem, the
Greek Americans of Boston do not reside in a propinquity
which would foster interaction with others of the same
origin. Hence, this associational function warrants
further consideration.

Individual Functions of Voluntary Associations

A survey of published descriptions of voluntary
associations leads to the conclusion that fundamentally
changed situations, whether social, cultural, political or
economic, stimulate persons to form and participate in
voluntary associations (Anderson 1966; Anderson and

Anderson 1958; Banton 1956; Banton 1957; Baskauskas 1971;
Brandel-Srier 1971; Comhaire 1950; Dotson 1965; Doughty
1969; 1970; Frankenberg 1957; Freedman 1967; Green 1969;
Hamer 1967; Handelman 1967; Hausknecht 1962; Hogg 1965;
Kapferer 1969; Kenny 1961; 1962; Leeds 1965; Levine 1965;
Little 1965; Mangin 1965; Meillasoux 1968; Noble 1970;
Norbeck 1966; Parkin 1966; Soen and De Camarmond 1972;
Treudley 1966; Wallerstein 1964; Wheeldon 1969). Melvin
Tumin (1957:33) contends that in the United States, sometimes termed the "nation of joiners," voluntary associations
have proliferated as a consequence of the competitive and
rapid upward social mobility which has always characterized
this society. Among other contributions voluntary associations assist Americans in their quest for upward social
mobility (instrumental), their adjustment to already
achieved social mobility (instrumental), and their
maintenance of attained social status (both symbolic and
instrumental). Elsewhere in the world, rural-urban migration or economic change in rural areas provide conditions
which result in the formation of numerous voluntary

associations. On the one hand, in such situations associations serve as substitutes for traditional institutions
which either have become dysfunctional for rural residents
or have not been transplanted into urban areas (both
instrumental). On the other hand, associations facilitate
personal adjustment to changed social and economic conditions (also instrumental). Invariably, wherever one
observes numerous voluntary associations in an area, major
social, cultural, political, or economic conditions have
been modified there with an attendant necessity for new
groupings which can satisfy human wants; as a consequence
it is these highly flexible organizations known as voluntary
associations which are formed.

Numerous social scientists who analyze the voluntary
associations which have arisen in African towns and Latin
American cities place their emphasis upon (1) needs which
kinsmen and long-term neighbors can no longer satisfy
according to traditional patterns and (2) the necessity of
adjusting to a strange and new urban industrial milieu.
In the words of Immanuel Wallerstein (1966:319) "the tribe

offered social security in the certainty of material
existence. . . . Migration out of the tribe upset these
assurances and diminished the individual's sense of social
and psychological security." As a consequence of this
rural-urban migration, both tribal and family ties weaken
but neither the urban employers nor the national govern-
ments have been able to satisfy the needs of urban workers
(Little 1965:47). Toward this end, numerous voluntary
associations are organized. Invariably the first associations to be organized are those which provide health or
bereavement benefits. Unlike marriage, one cannot postpone
illness or burial until his next journey home (Wallerstein
1966:320). For similar reasons, migrants also soon form
mutual aid, professional, and rotating credit associations
(Meillassoux 1968:74; Little 1965:48, 51). Furthermore,
however, necessary the instrumental functions of such
associations may be, members also require satisfaction of
emotional and psychological needs.

Urban associations are said to "cushion" the
changes imposed upon migrants.[2] In Paul Doughty's view

[2]For the case of Africa, W.T. Morrill goes so far as
to assert that "voluntary associations are one of the most
often used and most effective techniques for softening the
shock of transplantation from the certainties of tribal life
into the uncertainties of city life" (Morrill 1967:54).

(1970:40, 45; cf. Mangin 1965:318) migrant associations in Lima, Peru, are "actual extensions of the rural society and culture" which provide the migrants with a psychologically significant sense of continuity while they are striving to comprehend the strange urban environment. Toward this end, rural migrants residing in Lima have formed many associations, each of which recruits members who originated in the same areas of rural Peru. In addition to cementing group integration, these associations preserve traditional institutions such as the highly ritualized pattern for consumption of alcoholic beverages which Vogt (1970:14-16) and others have observed elsewhere in Latin American peasant communities. By preserving such aspects of a rural Peruvian community, associations in Lima offer the migrant a respite from the city's unfamiliarity, and whenever the uncertainties, strangeness, and frustrations of urban life become unbearable, the migrant can temporarily retreat to the premises of his association where he can be sure that some highland norms still prevail. Therefore, elements of continuity with past experiences as well as emotional

support from one's peers appears to facilitate migrants'
adjustments to urban life while providing expressive,
instrumental, and sociability functions.

Provisions for financial assistance, emotional
support, or a "cultural bridge" contribute toward the
adjustments of individuals who have been faced with a
changed milieu; however these services which voluntary
associations provide do not directly enhance members'
abilities to interact with employers and other strangers in
ways which both are culturally appropriate and have the
desired effects. As another individual instrumental
function of voluntary associations, participation in some
of these organizations socializes members to the norms of
the group. To illustrate, through involvement in their
voluntary associations rural migrants to Lima, Peru,
quickly learn the urban social meaning of coca chewing,
rural dress, and rural hair style. Because of sanctions
from their fellow members, recent migrants soon discontinue
practices which would advertise their rural origin and
therefore bring discrimination upon themselves (Mangin

1965:316).[3] Wallerstein, Little, Banton, Meillassoux,
Mangin, Treudley, and others suggest that the plethora of
offices in many associations permits members to learn and
practice modern modes of behavior. For example, Banton
(1968:360) observes that because of the fines which are
levied for late arrival at meetings, African migrants
become impressed with a need for punctuality; without
doubt, the observance of clock time which persons learn
can only benefit them in their urban employment. Indeed,
one might observe that the regular payment of dues, although
monetarily minimal, actually encourages some development
of thrift habits. Most importantly, during the time that
members pass from offices of little prestige to offices of
greater prestige, they also learn to perform tasks of
increasing complexity (Ibid.). Meillassoux and others
establish that through emphasis upon "proper" speech,
"proper" dress, and successful execution of leadership
roles, urban associations encourage and then reward members
for their cumulative adoption of city ways (1968:75-76).
Whether latent or manifest the instrumental achievements of

[3]Indeed, Mangin notes that at least one association
conducted a formal course in etiquette (1965:316).

such associations depend upon the expressive function--
members must derive some personal satisfactions while they
are, in effect, being trained in new modes of behavior.

Little observes that by providing a context in
which a set of differentiated urban roles may be learned,
participation in associations hastens the adjustments of
members to urban interaction (Little 1965:1). Starting with
only vague expectations about contacts with strangers,
African migrants usually first learn a few gross distinctions among tribesmen which are based upon geographical
separation of their origins as well as their cultural
similarities. The various statuses learned by members of
voluntary associations further provide more finely differentiated bases for social relations (Ibid.). But the urban
associations which most facilitate migrants' adaptation to
the city are not the most "modern" or the most Western in
orientation; they are syncretistic associations, emphasizing both the traditional and the modern (Hogg 1965:226).
Such "associations build for the rural migrant a cultural
bridge, conveying him from one kind of social universe to

another" without compeling him to abruptly transform
himself (Little 1965:1; 1971:12, 14).

Voluntary association membership may also provide
members with social prestige not otherwise attainable.
Furthermore, research in Africa and elsewhere demonstrates
that participation in voluntary associations can achieve
social, if not economic, mobility for both individuals and
groups. To this end, politically ambitious persons may
join in order to "learn how to speak" (Wallerstein 1964:
116). Moreover, persons lacking the education which is
necessary for economic mobility can become "prominent in
social activities" by contributing actively to the operation
of several associations (Brandel-Srier 1971:46; Koss 1965:
210). Even conflicts among association officers can have
the effect of providing "an essential platform on which
leaders could be seen to be active and exerting influence,
and their public performance could be observed, assessed,
criticized, and praised" (Wheeldon 1969:174-175). Therefore, conflicts among the leaders within an association may
offer necessary opportunities to persons who aspire to

"social prominence." From these data one concludes that if more traditional sources of self esteem become inoperative or competitions for upward social mobility become intense, voluntary association membership, in turn, functions as an essential source of self esteem.

Furthermore, because associational memberships usually crosscut other social groups, joiners discover that they can extend their social networks to include persons not otherwise accessible to them. Instances of this function are reported for Africa, Aruba, Peru, and the United States to name only a few locations. To illustrate, in Lima, Peru, it is largely through membership in regional associations that migrants are able to make valuable contacts with lawyers, politicians, doctors, and businessmen (Mangin 1965:317). Indeed, members who serve on committees also find that their horizons have been widened as a result of their frequent interactions with officials of the national and local government (Ibid.:316). Nevertheless, it is apparent that persons also participate in associations because their shared membership experiences can intensify already existing social bonds. In short, depending upon the local situation, associations appear to be sufficiently flexible that they can either stimulate members' incorporation into wider social networks or further intensify already established social relationships.

In descriptions of voluntary associations which anthropologists study several commonalities may frequently be discerned. To begin with, one finds numerous associations in areas where rural-urban or international migration has occurred. For individuals who have undergone such transplantations, membership in voluntary associations may (1) satisfy needs no longer traditionally provided for by kinsmen or long-term neighbors, or (2) facilitate adjustment to a strange and new urban environment. By providing a context in which a set of differentiated urban roles may be learned, participation in associations hastens the adjustments of members to urban interactions. But the urban associations which most facilitate migrants' adaptation to the city are not the most "modern" or the most "Western" in orientation; they are syncretistic associations which build a cultural bridge for the migrant by emphasizing both the traditional and the modern. Associations may also provide members with social prestige not otherwise attainable. Whether or not individuals join associations because of instrumental motivations, their participation can result in an expansion of their social networks or an intensification of already existing social bonds. In this dissertation I shall not only examine the pertinence of these functions to the Mexican Aztec Society of Bethlehem, Pennsylvania but also determine which additional functions this organization has served for either the membership body or particular members.

Hypothesized associational functions which are supported by empirical data and which are also relevant to the present study include each of the following general group functions: instrumental, expressive, sociability, and symbolic. One should note in passing that each function applies to individual members of associations as well as to social groups. Nevertheless, focusing upon group functions which are particular to Mexican American voluntary associations, researchers claim that these organizations provide for: (1) "the preservation of the general Mexican American way of life," (2) a variety of organizations to join, (3) "informational and communication networks," (4) a framework of cultural pluralism, and (5) interaction among Mexican Americans. Each shall be examined with respect to applicability in Bethlehem, Pennsylvania.

Changes Within Voluntary Associations

Because changes within either the organization, goals, or operation of the Mexican Aztec Society all influence the impact of this association upon Mexican American members, these transformations are given detailed examination in this dissertation. Moreover, I shall employ the "formalization" model devised by John Tsouderos (1953) as the primary vehicle for organizing and analyzing the events which transpired within the Mexican Aztec Society during its thirty-four years of existence.[4] Briefly stated, formalization encompasses the process by means of which informal voluntary associations successively acquire

[4]A more detailed definition of the "formalization process" appears in the introductory chapter.

elective leadership statuses, one or more professional
leadership positions, segmentation into various associations
which recognize a centralized organization, and a further
tightening of the central executives' control over constituent associations. In Tsouderos' view the principal
processes of formalization include unsustained initial
growth in the size of the membership body, conversion of
primary groups into secondary groups, increasing differentiation of member statuses, attenuation of communication
between members and officers, a growing disaffection of
members, and a decline in member participation if not an
eventual decrease in size of membership. Other writers
focus upon additional aspects of voluntary associations
but these variables are either subsumed by or compatible
with Tsouderos's model. However, in the case of the
Mexican Aztec Society other factors which are not directly
related to formalization, such as shifts in composition
of the membership body and goals of the organization, have
transformed this association's characteristics. Similarly,
although observed modifications in the functions which this

association has served for either individuals or groups do
not necessarily constitute formalization, they are nevertheless, examined in detail. Furthermore, in describing
interactions among Azteca members, I shall not only treat
the patterns of change, such as formalization, which
characterize the association's thirty-four year history but
also the continuities which are apparent for that period.

Mexican American Associational Activity

The Predominant View

Perhaps cherishing W. Lloyd Warner's statement
(1953:191; cf. Goldhamer 1951:592) that voluntary
associations "have been prominent and important features of
American life from the very beginnings of the Republic,"
various observers of Mexican Americans deny that members
of this group engage in associational activities. Although
decrying this attitude, Edward Casavantes (1971:48),
himself a Mexican American, concurs in his summary of the
views which social scientists frequently express. Nevertheless, some research supports the numerous subjective

impressions that the rate of Mexican American participation
in voluntary associations is less than that of the population of the United States taken as a whole. On the one
hand, Barbosa-Dasilva (1968:42) reports that only
approximately twenty percent of Mexican Americans join
associations. On the other hand, despite highly variable
results from investigations of the joining habits of
United States residents, nevertheless, the overall cal-
culated rate of participation is in the neighborhood of
fifty percent (Sills 1968:365). In Barbosa-Dasilva's
assessment some but not all of this difference in joining
can be explained by controlling for socioeconomic status
(1968:38). One may conclude from these observations that
proportionally fewer Mexican Americans join voluntary
associations than do other natives of this "land of
joiners"; a scientific explanation of the differential
joining habits appears in a later section.

One learns from published studies of Mexican
American voluntary associations, for example, that both
leaders and followers severely hamper the effective

operation of these organizations. To demonstrate this point for the topic of leadership, as a result of his research into Mexican American social action associations, Albert Sargis (1966:173) concludes that leaders cannot mobilize the members because the officers do not know how to communicate their programs for action. Elsewhere, as stated by the authors of a major work describing Mexican Americans (Grebler, Moore, and Guzman 1970:552), "Mexican American leaders are highly individualistic and competitive or often even hostile to one another." To researchers who accept this viewpoint, the competitiveness and hostility among leaders are seen to prevent effective cooperation both within and among Mexican American voluntary associations. As for the members, they are said to "begrudge success to their leaders," thus undermining them rather than cooperating (Ibid.). Consistent with the foregoing observations, Watson and Samora (1954:418) failed to discover a single person who was generally recognized as a leader in a population of 1450 Mexican Americans.

In addition to these pessimistic prospects for
Mexican American efforts at organization, one may further
observe that because of internal divisiveness (Alvarez
1971:69) those formal voluntary associations which have
been founded by Mexican Americans seldom long endure.

Cultural Determinism as Explanation
of Mexican American Associational
Problems

Various social scientists seek within traditional
Mexican American culture the cause of Mexican Americans'
alleged failure to effectively organize themselves into
enduring voluntary associations. To some writers, Mexican
American culture resembles a folk culture which, despite
appropriateness to some earlier milieu, cannot now be
adapted to an industrialized society (Watson and Samora
1954:317; Lane 1968:4-5). It is asserted that as one
aspect of this traditional culture, the cherished ideals
of individualism and family loyalty prevent development of
viable Mexican American voluntary associations (Sheldon
1970:127-128; Briegel 1970:161; Barbosa-Dasilva:34). Yet

paradoxically some of these scholars also claim a "rural folk distaste for individual advancement at the expense of one's peers" (Sheldon 1970:128) discourages Mexican Americans from developing and applying leadership skills. Furthermore, authors who espouse this viewpoint that Mexican American culture _is_ maladaptive, also deny that the members of this ethnic group can improve their positions through pluralistic culture change; instead the writers claim that only by a total rejection of their cultural heritage, can Mexican Americans improve their lot.

Most of these statements can be derived from the assumption that because of a static "traditional" Mexican American culture: (1) All Mexican Americans are highly individualistic and jealously guard their personal autonomy; (2) They envy and attempt to obstruct any other Mexican Americans who are becoming successful leaders (or businessmen); (3) Those Mexican Americans who distinguish themselves in politics or business did so by rejecting all of Mexican American culture, becoming instead "American."

Contrary Evidence[5]

Because of the absurdity of the assumption that
any culture could ever be static, I shall reject this
notion without belaboring the obvious.

During this century Mexican American populations
have not existed as unorganized aggregates. In the words
of Manuel Gamio (1969b:132), the Mexican anthropologist
who studied this topic during the 1920's,

> It is characteristic of the Mexican in his
> own country, especially in the small towns
> and rural regions, that he [does not]
> readily form cooperative organizations with
> his fellows for their mutual benefit. In
> this respect the immigrant in the United
> States changes radically. His social
> interests are aroused and develop markedly;
> the number of Mexican societies in the
> United States are a witness to this.

Indeed, wherever they have settled in the United States,

Mexican immigrants have formed numerous voluntary

---

[5]Because during the 1920's and the 1930's many
Mexicans residing in the United States were citizens of
Mexico, both terms "Mexican" and "Mexican American" are
employed in the discussion rather than solely the latter
label.

associations (<u>Ibid</u>.).[6] Therefore, based upon Gamio's

observations one must admit that Mexican American

associational activity represents an accommodation to

residence in the United States which is <u>not</u> derived from

"traditional Mexican culture."

Said to be unable to organize, Mexicans have

founded at least one formal voluntary association which

has been in continuous existence since 1894. At that time

---

[6]One can cite numerous publications in support of
Gamio's statement. Paul Lin (1963:92) states that in
Kansas City of 1920 there were seven Mexican American
voluntary associations, in addition to one founded in
1924 which has continued to the present. Paul Taylor
(1934:173) identifies twelve Mexican associations in
Corpus Christi, Texas of 1910 and seventeen associations
in Nueces County, Texas of 1917. Kathleen Gonzales
(1928:1;<u>cf</u>, Arnold 1928:10) reports that twelve Mexican
associations existed in San Antonio, Texas in 1928 and
one of those had six hundred members. For the same year
Paul Taylor (1932:131) identifies twenty-three in Chicago,
Illinois, eight in Indiana Harbor, Indiana; and four in
Gary, Indiana. Although others may have been ignored, he
describes one association which existed in the Imperial
Valley, California in 1927 (Taylor 1931a:63). Also, at
least one Mexican association in Omaha, Nebraska owned "a
large hall" in 1924. According to James Officer about
1929 the League of United Latin American Citizens (LULAC),
a Mexican defense association, extended its political
activities from Texas to several other states (1964:26).
In many of these cases the authors judge that they have
considerably underestimated the number of Mexican associations in the various areas; moreover, the sources cited
are only representative rather than exhaustive of the
available literature. In summary, the published accounts
do indeed suggest that Mexicans in the United States have
formed many voluntary associations, even during their
first years of residence in the United States.

Mexican American residents of Tucson, Arizona, founded the
Alianza Hispano Americana as a defense against Anglo
Americans. In the judgment of James Officer (1963:53-56),
an anthropologist who extensively studied Mexican American
associations in that city, the _Alianza_ and other instrumental associations later organized for defense _did_
successfully remedy the principal grievances of the
Mexican Americans. Because of the _Alianza_'s prior success
in combatting discrimination against Mexican Americans,
neither this or any other local Mexican American voluntary
association presently needs to function actively as a
defense association; instead other goals have since been
substituted (_Ibid_:365).

Despite obvious subjectivities on the part of
writers who describe Mexican Americans of the 1920's,
nearly all accounts admit the existence of one or more
voluntary associations wherever Mexicans settled. Some of
the associations, known as _honorificas_ however, are
characterized as "creatures of the Mexican consuls and
attract primarily those who are most sentimentally and

patriotically attached to Mexico herself" (Ibid.:29).
Each year these associations usually become active only in
time to hold celebrations for the two principal Mexican
patriotic holidays. Despite the fact that the members of
many honoríficas did not sustain a constant level of
activity throughout the year, the pervasiveness of these
associations, nevertheless, suggests that Mexican Americans
do marshall at least minimal ability to maintain organizations. One should also note that in most cases Mexican
Americans organized voluntary associations because of
individual motivations rather than as "puppets" of a
Mexican Consul General. Although evidence is lacking, the
formation and maintenance of honoríficas may have conveyed
the notion that voluntary associations provide legitimate
mechanisms for achievement of collective goals and
satisfaction of individual needs as well as provided a
context in which the statuses and roles necessary to the
functioning of voluntary associations might be learned and
developed.

Not only did Mexicans in the United States organize but they also did so for the express goal of modifying their economic environment. Many Mexican agricultural laborers were vulnerable to deportation because of their illegal entry to the United States. However, in the Southwest, they engaged in almost continual unionization and confrontation with growers from 1900 until World War II.[7] Indeed, Mexican American strike activities were geographically as widespread as the jobs which attracted Mexican Americans. As Romano (1968:15) observes,

> During the thirties . . . [agricultural]
> workers of Mexican descent were striking in
> Arizona, New Mexico, Texas, Idaho, Colorado,
> Washington, Michigan, as well as California.
> But Mexican farm workers were not alone in
> their union activities. Mexican sheepherders,
> pecan shellers, and coal miners also struck
> during the 1930's.

---

[7] Romano (1965:14-15) states that one union, La Confederacion de Uniones Obreras (Confederation of Workers' Unions), consisted of over three thousand members who were organized into twenty locals distributed throughout southern California. Five thousand agricultural laborers struck in the Imperial Valley, California in 1930 preceeding the strike of 1933 in which seven thousand Mexicans left the fields of Los Angeles County (Ibid.:15). In at least two other instances during the era, Mexicans in the Southwest either organized unions of five thousand or more members or staged strikes participated in by that number of Mexicans (Ibid.).

The notion of the passive Mexican peón who cannot create an organization and who will not accept another person's leadership is rendered inconsistent with documented Mexican and Mexican-American efforts at unionization.

Partially as a consequence of the new experiences of Mexican Americans who served as soldiers during World War II, soon after the cessation of hostilities, numerous politically active voluntary associations were formed. To illustrate, the American G.I. Forum was founded in Corpus Christi, Texas in response to a funeral director's refusal to bury a Mexican American war casualty. This association's concerted actions eventually led to interment of the deceased soldier in Arlington National Cemetery (Grebler et al.:542-543). Since that time this association has supported numerous other causes and its especially active branches are now located in Chicago, Detroit, Kansas City, and Denver. Furthermore the American G.I. Forum maintains a staff in Washington, D.C. in order to inform the membership of pertinent federal programs (Officer 1964: 27). Another association, Community Service Clubs,

Incorporated, is based in Denver and takes as its goal an
improvement in social and economic status of Mexican
Americans; the Unity League of Southern California was
organized for similar reasons (Ibid.:48). Other associations organized since World War II include the Mexican
American Political Association (MAPA), the Political
Association of Spanish Speaking Organizations (PASSO), and
the Community Service Organization (CSO) all of which have
attained an interstate membership. Grebler, Moore, and
Guzman observe that these more recent organizations have
become more effective than some earlier associations by
reducing their exclusivity: all classes, the foreign born,
and speakers both Spanish and English are eligible for
membership (Grebler, et al.:543). Furthermore, the spurt
of Mexican American associational activities which occurred
following World War II has been increasing since that time.

     Unionization efforts pioneered by Mexican Americans
decades earlier were renewed by the National Farm Workers
Union following World War II. During the 1950's, as well
as during the remainder of the 1940's, the Mexican American

members and leaders of the National Farm Workers Union
confronted Di Giorgio and other large produce growers with
demands, such as for supplies of potable water in the
fields. In the words of Ernesto Galarza (1970:4), author
of Spiders in the House and Workers in the Field and one
of the principal organizers, "The results were always the
same--small wage gains for the harvesters, the adamant
refusal of growers to recognize the union." Despite
decades of struggle, Mexican American labor unionists had
never won a major strike against the large agricultural
producers until in 1967 when agricultural workers organized
by César Chávez succeeded in unionizing the grape industry.
However, in order to gain that success they were compelled
to neutralize some of the power of growers by enlisting the
economic support of many non-Mexican Americans throughout
the country. In light of the relative advantages of
wealthy growers, it would be erroneous to blame any
"inability to organize" for the apparent failures of all
but one of the many Mexican American agricultural strikes.

Anthropological investigations of Mexican American voluntary associations in San Antonio, Texas and Tucson, Arizona have likewise produced evidence that members of this population should be credited with successful organizational activity. Based upon his study of one hundred forty-three Mexican American associations in San Antonio, J.H. Lane (1968:183) concludes that "the Mexican-American community in San Antonio is capable of producing the required leadership and followership." Mexican Americans maintain numerous voluntary associations in San Antonio; he estimates that more than five hundred of these organizations exist in that city (Ibid.:53). Furthermore, Lane also asserts (Ibid.:55) that "For an ethnic group that is persistently described as lacking in organizational capabilities, it would appear that there is a rich variety of association types among those Mexican Americans who do participate." Hence, Lane's data lead to the conclusion that Mexican Americans have indeed successfully organized and maintained numerous voluntary associations of varied types.

In contrast with studies which report a dearth of
Mexican American members of voluntary associations, James
Officer (1964:364) notes a "good to·excellent" representa-
tion of Mexican Americans in Tucson's "military experience
associations, satellite organizations of the Democratic
Party, team sports clubs, Catholic sodalities serving the
Mexican parishes and a few of the inter-parish associations,
labor unions, fraternal benefit societies, and social
affinity sodalities." For Tucson one must therefore reject
the stereotype that Mexican Americans join only honoríficas,
mutual benefit associations, or associations sponsored by
the Catholic Church. Furthermore, Officer also explains
(Ibid.:374) that Mexican Americans who have been active in
their group's political associations are in great demand
as officers of predominantly Anglo associations connected
with the Democratic Party--because of their political and
leadership skills.

Evidence that Mexican Americans have successfully
organized numerous voluntary associations inevitably brings
into question the cultural deterministic explanations of

the admittedly lower rates of associational participation
exhibited by this population. However, in order to explain
these joining habits one need not assume maladaptive
culture patterns or other generalizations of equally
questionable scientific validity. The sociologist, David
Sills (1968:366) states that "Membership in a voluntary
association is a form of social interaction, and people who
are deprived of a broad range of social interaction
(farmers, Negroes, immigrant Roman Catholics, widows) are
almost by definition less likely to belong to voluntary
associations." The Mexican Americans do clearly fit into
this category and therefore their participation rate
can be explained by external factors rather than by the
internal factor of deficiencies in traditional Mexican
American culture.

As demonstrated by the foregoing analysis of
Mexican American associational behavior, a substantial
case can be made for tentatively accepting the thesis of
Romano, Vaca, and Alvarez, and other Mexican American
authors that anthropologists have indeed perpetuated a

distorted view of Mexican American culture. Because the research presented herein documents the entire history of a successful Mexican American voluntary association (i.e., one which has survived for several decades), the data and analyses delineate in detail the behavior of Mexican Americans who have disproved, at least in Bethlehem, the statement that members of this ethnic group cannot long sustain voluntary associations. In addition to describing the associational behavior of Mexican Aztec Society members, I shall closely examine this association in order to determine the functions which it has served and also in order to test the utility of Tsouderos's formalization model of associational change. But to specify the conditions and events which led to the formation of the Mexican Aztec Society, I first describe Bethlehem, Pennsylvania and its Mexican colony.

CHAPTER II

BETHLEHEM AND ITS COLONIA

MEXICANA

The City of Bethlehem

Although initially attracted to Bethlehem by the
possibility of employment as industrial workers, once they
had settled there many aspects of immigrants' lives, in
addition to purely economic matters, became influenced by
the interplay of three salient characteristics of the
local social structure: the city's deep-seated sectionalism, the predominantly immigrant population of the south
side,[1] and the policies and immense power of the Bethlehem
Steel Corporation.

Bethlehem's long enduring sectionalism, which is
still observable, derives from 1740 at which time the
Moravians founded a communal settlement upon the northern
bank of the Lehigh River (Yates 1963:4). In an attempt to

---

[1] After 1917, when the boroughs of Bethlehem (north
of the river) and South Bethlehem (south of the river)
consolidated to become a single third class city, it
becomes appropriate to employ the designations of "north
side" and "south side."

avoid close contact with worldly outsiders, the Moravians
restricted any traders or others who passed through the
area to the opposite bank of the Lehigh River, thus setting
the stage there for later industrialization which was also
limited to South Bethlehem as the borough to the south of
the river came to be named (People of Bethlehem 1967:2).
Although no longer residing communally after the mid-
nineteenth century, Moravians continued to occupy
Bethlehem (the "north side") while industrialists and
immigrant ironworkers located in South Bethlehem (Ibid.:
3; Yates 1963:55). However, after some decades of
residence in South Bethlehem, immigrants or their descendants moved to the north side eventually to be followed by
members of yet more recently arrived immigrant groups.
Indeed, for over a century the pronounced sectionalism
which prevailed in the Bethlehem area has been characterized by relatively unacculturated ethnic groups of low
social status residing on the south side paralleled by
conservative Moravians and acculturated immigrants or their
descendants residing in the more prestigious north side.

Decades before the arrival of Mexicans, a pattern
had been set in which members of ethnic groups dwelt
exclusively on the south side, often in enclaves, while
laboring for the steel corporation. Indeed, during the
half century following the Civil War rapid expansion of
local iron and steel foundries depended upon the inexpensive labor provided by thousands of immigrants who settled
in South Bethlehem. In the score of years between 1890
and 1910 immigration caused the population of South
Bethlehem to double; and in 1910 immigrants and their
children accounted for seventy percent of the borough's
population (The People of Bethlehem 1967:6). Attracted by
wartime demands for laborers in the steel foundries additional thousands of Eastern European immigrants settled in
Bethlehem during World War I (Vadasz n.d.:7). By 1923,
when large numbers of Mexicans first detrained in
Bethlehem, the south side had been a municipality of
immigrants for several decades. Furthermore, as recently
as 1939 the following description applied to the south
side.

> Along Third Street are Greek restaurants,
> redolent with boiled lamb and syrupy
> coffee, Italian groceries with windows
> strung with fiery sausages and Parmigiono
> and Caciocavollo cheese; Russian tea houses
> and Roumanian restaurants amid Polish pool
> rooms and Hungarian societies. National,
> fraternal, and musical clubs flourish, and
> native costume celebrations of the various
> nationalistic groups are held with pomp
> and ceremony every Sunday during the summer
> in Central Park, and are known as 'Nationality
> Days' (Federal Writers Project 1939:147).

In other words, many ethnic groups were represented in

Bethlehem as were the yet more numerous ethnic voluntary

associations.

Between January and September of 1925 interviewers

from the Women's Bureau of the United States Department of

Labor contacted 1,026 female immigrant workers in the

Lehigh Valley (Manning 1930:132). Although results of this

study include data from the towns of Coplay, Palmerton, and

Allentown, as well as South Bethlehem and Northampton

Heights, the general picture of the immigrant workers'

life in the area during the 1920's is brought into high

relief. For example, many respondents reported that adverse

conditions in their homelands had precipitated their

emigration--"Times bad in old country, no land, no work,
no eat," "Ukrainians not make laws." Some adventurous
persons seem to have been caught up in 'emigration fever':
"everybody crazy to come to a better life." But by no
means did immigrants who settled in Bethlehem discover "the
promised land." Therefore, it is remarkable that almost
all of the women felt that their lot had improved as a
result of immigration to the United States. (Ibid.:21-22).
From the wealth of statistical data and case histories
collected by the Women's Bureau there emerges a pronounced
picture of industrial exploitation of laborers which can
be likened to the conditions in England which prevailed in
the early phases of the Industrial Revolution.

During Charles M. Schwab's presidency the South
Bethlehem plant of Bethlehem Steel became known as a
model of efficiency and economy in steel making. This
accomplishment derived in part from Schwab's knowledge of
technical processes, but in the main stemmed from his
notion that wages and productivity bore no relation to each
other. Under Schwab, Bethlehem's wages were the lowest in

the steel industry. For example, in 1909, when a minimum subsistence income level was $900, the average annual wage of Bethlehem Steel workers was $727.11; furthermore in 1910 a little over half of the men toiled twelve or more hours per day, and a seven day week, with no overtime pay for Sunday, was the lot of twenty-nine percent of the men (Vadasz n.d.:11-12). Fifteen years later working conditions had improved only slightly.

In 1925 the standard poverty level budget used by the Bethlehem Family Welfare Association in determining minimum needs for a family of five was $1,109.60 per annum (Manning 1930:98). About two-fifths of the families surveyed by the Women's Bureau had at least five members and about one-fourth had six or more (Ibid.:36). Those of the working women's husbands who were employed in the steel industry earned a median weekly wage of $24.90 ($1294.84 per annum given the improbable assumption of no losses in time) (Ibid.:47). Furthermore, the weekly wages of steelworkers were $1.90 less than the median wage for all employed husbands of working women who had jobs in the Lehigh

Valley (Ibid.). In other words, wages in other local
industries, such as textiles, automobile manufacture, and
cement, were higher than those paid by the most dominant
local industry (thirty-nine percent of the husbands sur-
veyed were employed in some aspect of steel manufacture)
(Ibid.). Furthermore, full employment--ideally five-and-
a-half ten hour days per week--was a rarity. Therefore,
because of inevitable illness as well as the probable
underemployment, steel workers residing in Bethlehem had to
earn more than their median wage in order to avoid poverty.
Given this economic situation, it is not surprising that
fully a third of the women in South Bethlehem worked; and
that when the work was available many worked longer hours
than the state legal maximum of ten hours per day (Ibid.:
96).

Once they were compelled to seek employment because
of economic adversity, many women experienced severe
hardship. Some case histories in the study report women
rising at 2:30 a.m. in order to do the family laundry
before the start of the working day or describe women as

hurrying off to the factories at 5 a.m. in order to produce
as much piecework possible. Other narratives tell of
textile workers' payments to skilled workers, such as
weavers, of as much as $20 (about one week's wages) for
the opportunity to learn to use particular machinery in
hopes of obtaining better jobs. Aged persons recount their
displacement by "young girls" hired to operate new machines;
persons who had been ill relate how their jobs were given
to others and the subsequent difficulty of finding new
employment. Furthermore, oftentimes children suffered
because of their mothers' employment: in one-quarter of
the homes working mothers were unable to provide adequate
supervision for their children not in school or for those
in school after school hours (Ibid.:42-43; passim). One
comes to see the Lehigh Valley in 1925 as a welter of human
suffering, privation, poverty, and misery.

Nevertheless, female immigrants utilized certain
strategies in order to make employment more bearable. More
than half of the women reported that the choice of a place
to ask for work was conditioned by the influences of

relatives, countrymen, or friends (Ibid.:104). Women who
had no such assistance in securing employment had a
difficult time finding a job. Many report that stumbling
upon shops where persons of similar ethnic background were
employed was the key to "getting a place" (Ibid.). Because
so many of the women employed in the Lehigh Valley--60.4
percent--did not speak English, the opportunity to
associate with fellow ethnics on the job greatly outweighed
adverse employment conditions (Ibid.:106). Once they had
found work many continued to work at the same place unless
difficulties over wages, shoddy materials, or frictions
with employers or fellow employees ensued (Ibid.:22).
However, women reported that conflicts often arose with
speakers of other languages. Noting a consequence of
ethnic social solidarity, in 1928 Paul Taylor's informants
stated that European foremen reserved for their own countrymen the best paying and least dangerous jobs (1931b:15).
Indeed, a general impression readily derived from these
studies is that during the 1920's the people of Bethlehem's

south side sorted themselves out in terms of ethnic identification in almost all contexts.

The immigrants who settled in Bethlehem encountered a foreign society as well as a strange industrial economy. Also, immigrants soon discovered that they occupied the lowest local socioeconomic stratum: "Neither the old families nor Americans from other parts of the country cared to associate with the immigrants" (Yates 1963:175). Given this exclusiveness of "Americans," immigrants had little choice but to seek out fellow members of their ethnic groups for social interaction. Indeed, as immigrants of each ethnic group settled in South Bethlehem a consistent pattern emerged. In contrast to the religious institutions of groups already in residence--Moravians, 'Pennsylvania Germans,' Welsh, and English--the Irish and subsequent groups established national parishes. ". . . all the European nationality groups organized through their church using that medium as their major contact with other groups in the community" (People of Bethlehem 1967:5). Under religious auspices parochial schools (in some cases) and voluntary associations based on common ethnicity soon

followed (Yates 1963:176).

> To the people of South Bethlehem, therefore,
> the church during this period became more than
> just a religious body. It provided a social,
> fraternal, and political framework to keep
> each of the various ethnic groups united in an
> effort to resist assimilation and Americaniza-
> tion. The church became the place where the
> national language was spoken and where the
> children were educated in the ways of the 'old
> country' (People of Bethlehem 1967:5-6).

After having established national parishes, the various

ethnic groups formed their own voluntary associations,

perhaps in emulation of those so prevalent in higher social

strata (Beard and Beard 1930:730-731; Yates 1963:177):

"Often . . . the social organizations of the immigrants

began through a connection with the church, for example,

the various Sokols and beneficial societies (Yates 1963:

176). National churches, thus constituted the bases from

which voluntary associations of fellow ethnics were derived.[2]

---

[2]National churches established in Bethlehem include
Sts. Cyril and Methodius (Slovakian, 1891); St. John
Capistrano (Magyar, 1903); St. Stanislaus (Polish, 1905);
Holy Rosary (Italian, 1902); First Slovenian Wendic (1914);
Saint Nicholas Orthodox (Russian); Sts. Peter and Paul
(Greek Orthodox); and St. Josephat (Ukrainian). Holy
Infancy Roman Catholic Church, had been established by the
Irish at the beginning of the last third of the nineteenth
century; the Ibero-American Congregation was established
there in 1930, to serve the Spanish, Portuguese, and
Mexicans who had settled in Bethlehem after the First
World War.

Taken together, the ethnic voluntary associations, whether independent or church sponsored, provided for financial assistance, sociability, spiritual resources, and maintenance of group identity as well as serving as agencies mediating between immigrants and other groups or institutions in Bethlehem.

Executives of the Bethlehem Steel Corporation, especially President Charles M. Schwab, perceived that their company would benefit from the maintenance of barriers between ethnic groups. Formerly a protege of Andrew Carnegie, who is said to have advocated the employment of diverse ethnic groups because "they fight each other, not the company," Schwab had doubtlessly realized the importance of ethnic church membership to the steelworkers because for several years prior to the strike of 1910 the Corporation had aided in the perpetuation of ethnic barriers by carefully deducting the workmen's church dues directly from their pay envelopes and disbursing the collections to the appropriate parish priests (Vadasz 1967:23). This corporate policy guaranteed Schwab that he could extend some influence

upon his workers through the personages of their clerics.
Indeed, much of Schwab's success in quelling the strike of
1910 may be attributed to his ability to manipulate the
influential leaders of each ethnic group (Vadasz 1967:
22-23, 36).

Following this strike Schwab then took action to
insure that in the event of another strike his thousands
of immigrant employees would no longer be able to enlist
the support of South Bethlehem's borough officials as they
had in 1910. In 1917, as a result of Schwab's efforts to
minimize the effects of the borough's solidarity, South
Bethlehem was joined to the boroughs of West Bethlehem and
Bethlehem (which had merged in 1904), beginning a trend
toward lessening the parochial sectionalism which marked
the relationships among these contiguous municipalities
(Vadasz n.d.:7; People of Bethlehem 1967:5). Formation of
a third class city, with a smaller administrative council
than that of either of the two pre-existing boroughs, would
require candidates for political office to mount expensive,
city-wide campaigns for office, resulting in the elimination

of politicians whose beliefs were not shared by "native Americans"--which beliefs were in consonance with those of the Bethlehem Steel Corporation officials (Vadasz n.d.:7). In the new city the solidarity of the ethnic groups of the south side would be counter-balanced, if not outweighed, by the solidarity of the conservative north side. In short, Schwab desired to lessen the possibility that official municipal sentiments again would be contrary to the goals of the Steel Corporation's directors.

In contrast with the protracted strike of 1910, the strike of 1919 lasted but ten days.[3] President Grace, who had succeeded Schwab, successfully manipulated the ethnic steelworkers into not joining the strikers--thus insuring the strike's failure (Vadasz n.d.:14). Along with other measures, in order to promote the loyalty and solidarity of the work force vis-a-vis the company, the Corporation had already patriotically sponsored

---

[3]In the next twenty years organized labor had a difficult time in Bethlehem's steel industry. Eventually the Corporation partially capitulated, and permitted a company controlled union to function. During the depression union organizers again directed their activities toward the Lehigh Valley, but the United Steelworkers of America was not recognized as a collective bargaining agent for local steelworkers until 1941 (Vadasz n.d.:14).

naturalization classes and paternalisitically established
real estate agencies through which employees might purchase
houses, processes which effectively entwined the steelworkers interests with national interests as well as those
of the steel company (Vadasz n.d.:16-17). It is again
apparent that the Corporation officials had great insight
into the local social system. Recognizing the value of
group activities and voluntary associations to local
residents, soon after the abortive strike the company band
was made available for free concerts in the park and
offered its services, gratis, for street dances; a company
soccer team and gymnasium for boxing were publicized; and a
company-financed chess and checkers club was established
(Ibid.:19). Considering the nature of these fringe
benefits, on the one hand, Corporation officials sought to
undermine the influence of ethnic voluntary associations
upon immigrant steelworkers, and, on the other hand, they
sought to gain the loyalty of workers by implementing
paternalistic measures.

Arrival of Mexicans and their Early Experiences

As a result of recruitment of Mexican laborers by the Bethlehem Steel Corporation, a direct response to the acute labor shortage existing in Pennsylvania at that time, a total of nine hundred and forty-eight Mexicans arrived in Bethlehem between April 6th and May 30, 1923; nine hundred and twelve men, twenty-nine women, and seven children (Bethlehem Globe-Times a; Taylor 1931b:3).[4] Based upon data published by the Bethlehem Globe Times and other newspapers, one may conclude that the Mexicans' reception by local residents was far from cordial. Indeed, the following news item reflects negative attitudes about the advent of Mexicans.

> This tranquil Moravian city has been surprised over night by a veritable invasion of Mexican and Indian laborers, who have been brought to this town in three long trains, exciting the curiosity of the local population with their characteristic clothing and their broad palm sombreros. This invasion of Mexican laborers has given rise to many comments, and the laboring element here is asking itself thoughtfully what will be the significance of this

[4]Taylor made three visits to Bethlehem, between early 1928 and early 1930, of unspecified length.

immigration to the industrial future of
the city . . . [emphasis mine].[5]

The possibility is implied that steelworkers viewed with

alarm this supposed "invasion" of one thousand laborers

who, indeed, might have potentially been willing to under-

mine the existing wage structure. It would appear that

the working class residents of Bethlehem originally

opposed the entry of Mexicans into the local labor market.

In spite of the fact that no strike seems actually to have

been called in 1923, Paul Taylor (1931b:13) suggests that

the Mexicans were first viewed by the other workers as

"strikebreakers" or laborers whose presence would permit

a cut in wages. This mistaken notion may indicate that

the strikes of 1910 and 1919 had not been forgotten.

Interestingly enough, one local academic has described a

photograph of a group of Mexicans detraining in 1923 which

shows the Mexicans marching between two lines of policemen.[6]

---

[5]In apparent error Paul Taylor (1931b:5) cites La
Prensa as the source of this clipping. Also, one can assume
that the reporter used the term "Indian" because of physical
traits rather than cultural traits.

[6]This photograph, which I was unable to view, may
have recorded an arrival of Mexicans which was also described by a Globe-Times reporter. The article states that
the train was met by "a detail of police under Lieutenant
Lucas." The four hundred arrivals are included in the
nine hundred forty-eight Mexicans recruited by the Bethlehem
Steel Corporation (Bethlehem Globe-Times b).

One amateur historian, who claims knowledge of local
immigrant groups, explains that rather than being present
for the protection of onlookers from the newly-arrived
Mexicans, the policemen were actually deployed in order to
protect the Mexicans from the onlookers. Moreover,
attitudes of south side residents were such that many
ethnic groups derived much of their acceptance from the
fact that most male members were both married and residing
with their spouses. Little wonder, then, that when over
nine hundred Mexican males arrived in 1923, their advent
was hardly welcomed with warmth. Such statements by non-
Mexicans, combined with journalistic accounts and the
reports of second generation Mexican Americans about the
experiences of their parents, indicate that the Mexicans
faced considerable initial hostility from local residents;
in contrast, however, today most "old-timers" idealize
their initial reception in the city.

Although the arrival of Mexicans in Bethlehem was
little noted by reporters except for a brief note on the
financial page, by the end of their first week in that city

the press had already begun to stereotype the Mexicans'
behavior. Several Mexicans, who apparently worked in the
Coke Works, were purported to have visited nearby
Hellertown where they "built a fire into the street and
intended occupying a vacant house." Hellertown's Chief
of Police responded by sending them home on the trolley,
promising to arrest them if the escapade were repeated
(Bethlehem Globe-Times c). One might question precisely
what message was communicated to the Mexicans; however,
this encounter must have encouraged Mexicans to confine
their social interactions to their countrymen.

Once the Mexicans had settled into their new
homes in Bethlehem, the Globe-Times seldom mentioned them
except when reporting incidents of violence and other
events in keeping with the sensationalism typical of
journalism in the 1920's. For instance, a "FIRE IN [the]
MEXICAN COLONY" caused by one Mexican smoking in bed rated
more newspaper coverage in the Globe-Times than that which
had been devoted to the arrival of a trainload of four
hundred Mexican laborers. Yet one does learn from this

article that in the area in which the fire occurred, Northampton Heights, the Mexicans were housed in barracks partitioned into rooms; each room contained bunks for twenty men (Ibid.d). About a week after this article appeared, the Globe-Times detailed a stabbing incident which took place in a barracks in Northampton Heights, perhaps because this event reinforced the popularly-held belief that Mexicans frequently engaged in knife-fighting as a matter of course (Ibid. e). After another Mexican allegedly inflicted upon a Negro "eight slight cuts on his face and arms," the front page caption read: "CAN'T FIND BAD MEXICAN [emphasis mine]."[7] In this case not only is one led to assume the Mexican's guilt prior to the outcome of a fair trial, but he is also publically branded as "bad" by the Bethlehem Globe-Times.

In still another article, the list of persons charged with gambling in Northampton Heights includes such a large proportion of Spanish surnames that, by implication

---

[7]While reading "A Costly Celebration" (Bethlehem Globe-Times f) one wonders if a blond-haired, blue-eyed Anglo would have been arrested only thirty minutes after midnight while "shooting in the New Year." In any case a Mexican was fined $25 for this offense in addition to having his newly-purchased $20 pistol confiscated by the police.

the Mexicans seem to have been deeply implicated in local vice (Bethlehem Globe-Times g). Additionally, this account also provides evidence for a continuing lack of communication between Mexicans and other groups--the Spanish names of the men are misspelled almost beyond recognition.

One reported incident is especially noteworthy because an informant today recalls details not known to the newspaper's reporter.

DRUNKEN MEXICAN GOES ON RAMPAGE WITH GUN

_____. a Mexican, residing in the camp at the Coke Works, drank moonshine Thursday night and then ran amuck with a revolver. The intoxicated Mexican fired several shots in the air and later sent a bullet in the direction of members of his family and wounded his eight year old son, _____, in the back and then shot himself through the hand . . . _____ also suffered from cuts from glass which he broke out of a door. Several persons informed the police that he was drunk and terrorized the community. _____ said that _____ chased her and others out of her home at the point of a gun (Ibid. h).

In the ethnographer's analysis it is apparent that the protagonist in this drama, whom I will call Raul Martinez,

was celebrating the Mexican Independence Day of September
16; perhaps he had begun celebrating on the previous day,
September 15, when members of the colonia mexicana held a
dance in commemoration of their patriotic holiday (Ibid. i).
Nevertheless, the day's events were memorable to one
informant who, forty-four years later, described them as
follows:

> Raul Martinez liked to drink. One day when
> he came home drunk his wife locked him out.
> When Raul broke in the house, his oldest boy
> was afraid and ran to hide under the bed.
> But when Raul saw someone crawl under the bed,
> he thought that his wife had a man in the
> house so he got out his pistol and shot at
> him. And he shot his eight year old son in
> the rear end.

Still other newspaper accounts which deal with
Mexicans report accidents and injuries or instances of
deviant behavior. Only in one case is there a note of
praise for a Mexican--a man whose "heroic efforts" to
fight a fire resulted in injuries which necessitated his
hospitalization (Ibid. j). In other words, in the fifteen
years following 1923 for which a sample of local newspapers

was read, only one news item was detected which relates a positive achievement on the part of a Mexican.

Rather than being atypical, the content and journalistic style of these accounts typifies the majority of newspaper articles which deal with Mexicans during the dozen years following 1923. Although the precise factual accuracy of any particular news article, as well as the neutrality of the reporter and the completeness of his account, can easily be called into question, the major contribution of these data stems from the clear implication that Mexicans were indeed made to suffer social stigma because of their national origin.

There are also indications that the Steel Corporation's executives stereotyped the Mexican laborers' ability to "endure heat," probably because of the confounding notions that all of Mexico is a tropical country and the people of the tropics can endure intense heat. Hence, they were assigned jobs in the Coke Works or near the blast furnaces and open hearths because they could "take it." Even though most of the Mexicans came from the Mesa Central, where winters are severe, it was thought that they "can't stand cold" (Taylor 1931b:14).

Epithets such as "dirty Mex" or "greaser" appear to have been fairly common in Bethlehem during the 1920's. Some Mexican Americans explain the discrimination directed against them by describing the demographic composition of the colonia mexicana in 1923: the vast majority were rather footloose unmarried males in their twenties. Most were former peasants with little formal education. Although many Mexicans in Bethlehem had been attracted to Pennsylvania by possible adventures, others had also fled Mexico as fugitives from either civil or military law. Thus, it is hardly surprising that during the 1920's the people of Bethlehem subscribed to a stereotype of Mexicans as dark-eyed bandits who were prone to knife fights and who had a penchant for gambling--in other words, persons who in general manifested behavior inappropriate to their host's culture. In fact, the numerous articles which appear in the Bethlehem Globe Times which mention the Mexicans strongly support and perpetuate this notion.

However, with few exceptions, the reflections of
Mexican American informants substantiate Taylor's observation that the Mexicans residing in Bethlehem met with far
less discrimination than the Mexicans who had located in
the Southwest. In all probability this comparison was true
of Bethlehem relative to the Southwest, but too large a
number of second-generation Mexican Americans remember the
discrimination which had existed a number of years ago for
there to have been no discrimination locally. However,
discriminatory statements such as that made by one Steel
Corporation executive, ranking the Mexicans above the
Slovaks and Windish in intelligence and his comment, "If
some people think the Mexicans are dumb, they should see
some of our Irish," are indicative of the ethnic stereo-
typing generally experienced by members of immigrant groups
in Bethlehem as late as 1930 (Taylor 1931b:13).

Although relocation to Bethlehem must have been
disruptive for the Mexicans, elderly informants choose to
recount their less unpleasant experiences. To illustrate,
a first generation Mexican American with particularly

sharp recall members the first verse of the corrido (folk
ballad) which was composed to commemorate the journey from
San Antonio to Bethlehem. Although the informant had
heard this corrido only once, in 1923, his rendition
corresponds closely to the first verse of the ballad
published by Paul Taylor (1931b:viii) under the name
Corrido Pensilvanio.

> On the twenty-eighth of April
> At six o'clock in the morning
> We set out under contract
> For the State of Pennsylvania

Points which the troubadour saw as sufficiently important
to record were the disinclination of the Mexicans to pick
cotton in Texas and the rule that most men could not travel
with their wives or sweethearts. Moreover, according to
the corrido, some Mexicans responded to the machinery in
the steel mills with such shock that they fled at "eighty
miles an hour" (Ibid.:ix). Although Mexican informants
apparently suppress any memory of culture shock long past,
the Corrido Pensilvanio, recorded during the 1920's,
preserves intact the evidence of intense anxieties which
stimulated many Mexicans to return to their homeland.

Initially the Bethlehem Steel Corporation had offered Mexicans the option of taking room and board in company-managed facilities, but after a year's time it no longer employed Mexican cooks nor provided board (Taylor 1931b:12). In fact, some Mexican families used this opportunity to become petit entrepreneurs by providing board tables for their countrymen who were unmarried or whose wives resided in Mexico. One Mexican woman recalls that she "boarded" ninety-five men while having the help of only one assistant. Although some unmarried Mexican males banded together for the purpose of accomplishing the necessary domestic chores, others decided that Bethlehem would be more to their liking if they were each able to depend upon a spouse who could prepare genuine Mexican meals.

Some Mexicans held that they could better withstand the rigors of steelwork if they regularly ate Mexican food. For this reason many Mexican males worked in Bethlehem for a year or two in order to amass the funds necessary for them to return to their villages and marry their novias (sweethearts)

who they had left behind. These men then accompanied their
brides to Pennsylvania. Similarly, married men who had
migrated alone to the United States also returned to Mexico
and brought their families back to Bethlehem. That a visit
to Mexico in search of a conjugal partner was a prevalent
pattern during the 1920's may be inferred by two observations. In 1923, only three percent of the Mexicans were
females. However, of the male first-generation Mexican
Americans who remained in Bethlehem, over sixty percent
married Mexican nationals.[8] In short, many Mexican males
adapted to the small size of their colonia and the near
non-existence of Mexican females in the colonia by
traveling to Mexico in search of conjugal partners.

For example, one particular informant, Juan Rivera,
related that he had a novia in 1923 when he migrated from
Jalisco, Mexico to Bethlehem, Pennsylvania. Until 1928
this man accumulated savings while working as a steelworker
and made the journey to Mexico only after writing to his
kinsmen in order to inquire as to whether his novia had
remained "true" to him. According to Rivera, he carried

[8]The first of these statistics is based upon
Taylor's data (1931b:3). The second statistic derives from
a census of the Mexican Americans which was prepared by
several informants in 1970.

expensive clothing and considerable cash which he spent on
several parties and a honeymoon in Mexico City. Suddenly
insolvent, Rivera was forced to borrow 200 pesos ($100)
from his brother, but this sum only conveyed the couple as
far as Chicago. He then pawned his watch and overcoat,
telegraphed a friend in Bethlehem requesting assistance,
and subsisted for a week using the cash which he had
obtained from the pawnshop. After receiving the loan from
his friend, Mr. and Mrs. Rivera proceeded to Bethlehem
where they lived for several months with the same friend,
who eventually became their compadre (co-godfather).

Although after the first year the Bethlehem Steel
Corporation ceased to provide board for the Mexican
steelworkers, until 1939 the company did continue to
provide them with living quarters. Known as the Labor
Camp, these facilities consisted of barracks and two-family
frame dwellings located on the grounds of the Corporation's
Coke Works and near the borough of Hellertown. Although
labor camps had long been utilized by American agricultural
growers and industrialists, the decision to provide dwellings

for Mexicans is entirely consistent with the steel company's
policy of attempting to forestall successful unionization
of workers by enmeshing employees in various quasi-
paternalistic programs.

Taylor describes a Mexican practice which has all
but disappeared by 1970. During the 1920's Mexicans
residing in Bethlehem assisted their relatives in emigrat-
ing from Mexico, the most notable illustration being that
of the man who thus aided over thirty consanguineal and
affinal kinsmen (Taylor 1931b:11). If the case of Fidel
Suarez is typical, the Mexicans would have assisted many
more kinsmen who wished to emigrate to the United States
were it not for the occurrence of the Great Depression.
Within two years of his arrival in 1923, Suarez had arranged
for the immigration of two brothers and one cousin. By
1929 Suarez had assisted five of eight siblings in their
migration to Bethlehem; however it was the depression which
prevented him from achieving his goal of amassing sufficient
funds to bring his entire nuclear family to the United
States.

If the figures provided by Paul Taylor may be
accepted as approximately accurate, the colonia mexicana
progressively declined in size from 1923 until 1930. In
fact, the month in which the largest number of Mexicans was
employed by the Bethlehem Steel Corporation, May of 1923,
was the month in which the Corporation's representatives
completed the recruitment program in San Antonio; in that
month 790 Mexicans received paychecks for their work in
the steel plant. Apparently, slightly over one hundred
Mexicans had already terminated their employment as
steelworkers. Moreover, in every month of the following
year, approximately fifty-eight of these Mexicans left the
Bethlehem Steel Corporation, with the number of Mexicans
employed remaining stable only during the three winter
months.[9] Thus, by May of 1924, only 232 Mexicans labored
for the Corporation; nonetheless, although the number of
Mexicans so employed had diminished to approximately 125
in 1930, in Taylor's estimation (Ibid.:1, 11-12) by that

[9]Calculated from Taylor's figures. Also, when the
monthly employment figures are plotted, the number of
Mexicans employed exhibits a constant rate of decline with
the passage of time (1931b:11).

time the total size of the colony itself had more or less
stablized at about 375.[10]

Without doubt, additional Mexicans repatriated to
their homeland during the Great Depression--a time when
thousands of their countrymen who had been living in the
United States also returned home. However, no quantitative
data are available for Bethlehem concerning this return
migration, although some informants place the magnitude at
fifty percent. Few Mexicans who weathered the Great
Depression in Bethlehem were inclined to depart during the
economically-booming war era which followed. Informants
recall that after World War II a number of Mexicans again
decided to postpone long-awaited returns to Mexico--which
they had been talking about at least since 1928--until
after their retirements in order to do so while receiving
pension checks.

From his study of records provided by the Bethlehem
Steel Corporation, Taylor establishes that most Mexicans

---

[10]The "size of the Mexican colony" of course
included dependents and others not employed by the Bethlehem
Steel Corporation. Also, because the figures for 1923 are
based only upon Mexicans recruited in San Antonio, the
total number of Mexicans employed is actually larger due
to the unspecified number of persons who independently
traveled to Bethlehem at a later date.

who were hired during the 1920's had lived in the United States for less than one year (Ibid.:8).[11] Also, Taylor's data lead to the conclusion that the Mexicans who migrated to Bethlehem were in their early twenties at the time of migration (Ibid.:8). In addition, he states that sixty percent of the Mexican laborers were married at the time that they became steelworkers. Doubtlessly, more than sixty percent had married by 1930 (Ibid.:9). Furthermore, Taylor remarks upon the conditions favoring group exogamy-- disproportion of the sexes, a stated absence of discrimination, and the small size of the Mexican population; in 1930 he reports no exogamous marriages of female Mexicans and only a handful of exogamous marriages of male Mexicans (Ibid.:27).

The observations of Taylor, Manning, and Vadasz lead to the conclusion that categories of ethnicity provided a major basis for the social interactions of Mexicans during the 1920's.

From the available evidence, Mexicans developed distinct relationships with the "Americans," the Negroes,

[11]Furthermore, the Cristero Rebellion in Mexico also stimulated migration to the United States.

the Poles, the Irish, the Spaniards, and various immigrant groups not here named. Apparently, the category labeled "Americans" consisted of all citizens of the United States who were neither recent immigrants or Negroes. To Europeans and "Americans" the Mexicans of 1930 reserved the label of Blanco (white) (Taylor 1931b:17). Nevertheless, although the Mexicans by implication classified themselves as non-white, they showed their distaste for the small Negro population (also non-white) by denhing to Negroes membership in the Mexican voluntary associations.

Paul Taylor reports that Mexicans experienced considerable friction, the cause of which is unexplained, with members of one particular ethnic group, the Poles. He notes that although Mexicans attended social events sponsored by the voluntary associations of numerous ethnic groups, they never attended events held at the Polish club (Taylor 1931b:21). Elsewhere, however, Taylor states that some solos (Mexican bachelors) boarded with Polish, Windish, Slovak, Spanish, and Mexican families (Ibid.:12).

To the Mexicans ethnicity also influenced their experience as steelworkers. By the 1920's, perhaps as the aftermath of the ethnic solidarity manifested by the strike of 1910, steel company executives had chosen to "split up" various ethnic groups: the "nationalities" were dispersed among various work groups, with a "neutral American" over them; if there were a foreman from one particular ethnic group on one shift, a person from a different ethnic group would be foreman on the next shift. Because it was thought that a foreman would favor his own countrymen, thus compelling workers of other ethnic groups to work harder, the Corporation executives interviewed by Taylor admitted that such a procedure gave "better control" over the men (Ibid.:15). Nevertheless, the Mexicans felt that "the company" did not discriminate against them; in their view "the company" consisted of "American" superintendents and executives. No doubt this sharp cognitive distinction between "Americans" and European "immigrants" reflects differences in the Mexicans' encounters with these two categories of persons.

Within a religious context, considerable friction
occurred between the Mexicans and the Irish, who had
founded Holy Infancy Roman Catholic Church. During the
late 1920's many Mexicans were encouraged to attend the
special Mass—celebrated in the church's basement—which
was officiated by Father Cordova, a Spaniard who had served
as a chaplain in Mexico. After several decades of residence in the United States, both Irish parishioners and
clergymen had lost their empathy with the more recently
arrived immigrants. It is said that because of Father
Cordova's difficulties with the Irish pastors, the Bishop
had been forced to place Father Cordova in an independent
position in the parish, directing a mission serving the
"Ibero-American Congregation of Holy Infancy Church."

During the 1920's the Mexicans maintained their
warmest relationship with residents of the local Spanish
colonia. To illustrate, a number of Mexicans belonged to
the Spanish voluntary association; however no Spaniards,
although eligible, elected to join the Mexican association
(Taylor 1931b:21). One can only speculate as to the degree

to which this situation is analogous to the present situation in which many Puerto Ricans belong to the Azteca but
few Mexican Americans belong to the Puerto Rican Beneficial
Society. It is possible that the Mexicans of the 1920's
and the Puerto Ricans of 1970 seek prestige through contact
with members of a higher status group.

In any case, the saliency of ethnicity as a basis
for differentiating among individuals suggest that particular behavioral expectations followed for each ethnic
category. Furthermore, Mexicans may have had to depend
upon cues of ethnicity because they interacted most frequently with fellow Mexicans and therefore little understood
non-Mexicans.

Life in the Labor Camp

During interviews with Mexican Americans aged
forty or more years, the informants usually broach the
subject of their life in the Bethlehem Steel Corporation's
Labor Camp.[12] Most first or second generation Mexican

---

[12]As an institution which ceased to exist a generation ago--which in fact existed only for one generation--
the Corporation's Labor Camp almost eludes complete and
objective description. Therefore, the account which
follows perforce depends upon oral history and memories of
Mexicans to a greater extent than it utilizes historical
records. For the same reason, most statements refer to

Americans either indicate that residence in the labor camp strongly influenced them in some significant respect or else express the intense feelings--positive or negative-- which they hold toward the company camp. In other words, when they reminisce about the period between 1923 and 1939 they invariably mention the labor camp in some context or other. It is the purpose of this section to explore the impact of that particular period upon the Mexican American's formation of voluntary associations.

General Description of the Labor Camp

The origin of this camp clearly lies in the acute labor needs of the steel industry which prevailed during World War I and the need to provide temporary housing for the immigrant laborers hired by the corporation at

---

the 1930's rather than the 1920's. Due to the general lack of interest in the Mexicans on the part of other residents of Bethlehem in all likelihood the Bethlehem Steel Corporation, which built and later demolished the Labor Camp, is the only repository of primary historical materials concerning this camp. However, the Corporation's lack of assistance to the researcher on this topic suggests a desire to forget that the Camp had ever existed. This attitude contrasts ironically, however, with that of the many Mexicans who favorably remember the Labor Camp and the paternalism of the company with great nostalgia.

that time.[13] At least two accounts place the founding of
Bethlehem's camp at 1915 or earlier (Daday 1966:8).[14] one
informant, who lived there as a child, states that although
the Mexicans always shared the camp with families of other
nationalities--Slavish, Hungarian, Portuguese, Polish, and
Spanish--Mexicans numerically predominated (Minority Life
1963:2). However, with the passage of time this predomin-
ance diminished as Mexicans found housing elsewhere and as
persons of other nationalities moved into the camp.[15] An
informant estimates that at any one time the residents of
the Labor Camp numbered about thirty-three families plus a
number of bachelors, totaling approximately two hundred to
two hundred and fifty residents; Paul Taylor reports that

---

[13]The construction of a labor camp was by no means
an innovation of the Bethlehem Steel Corporation. Both
steel companies and railroads had relied upon this arrange-
ment for decades.

[14]Daday appears to have quoted this paper (Minority
Life 1963:1) but he neglects to cite any sources. The
author of this paper, himself a second generation Mexican
American who had lived in the Labor Camp, supplemented his
own recollections by interviewing his kinsmen and other
first generation Mexican Americans.

[15]Although no precise data are available concerning the relative numbers of Mexicans residing in the Labor
Camp as opposed to those living elsewhere, Mexican "old
timers" estimate that two-thirds of their countrymen
resided in the camp during the 1920's but that the proportion declined to approximately one-third during the
succeeding decade.

in early 1929, seventeen families with fifty-six children plus thirty-four <u>solos</u>--one hundred and twenty-four Mexicans, resided in the Labor Camp (Taylor 1931b:12). Thus, although the Labor Camp corresponded in size to tiny villages in Mexico from which had come many of the Mexicans, the camp was by no means ethnically homogeneous. Furthermore, had it housed thousands of persons, one suspects that the residents might not now fondly remember the camp's familism.

One Mexican American describes life in the camp in a paper written for a sociology class held at Lehigh University. He relates that the housing consisted of either six-room frame dwellings or large barracks. To provide housing for small families some structures were partitioned into two apartments of three rooms each. Larger families generally rented an entire house, initially at a cost of $8.00 per month. (Eventually the cost of rent rose to $18.00 per month.) Says the Mexican American writer, "The homes for families contained good furniture, stoves--some provided by the Steel Company, good kitchen

sinks, electricity, and running water" (Minority Life
1963:2). Verbal statements by other informants indicate
that during the 1920's the facilities in the Labor Camp
were of a most rudimentary nature. To illustrate, even as
late as 1928 everyone had to stand in line for water from
the camp's single spigot. Over the ensuing years, however,
most families were able to install plumbing, at their own
expense. Nevertheless, at the same time the general
condition of the camp's frame buildings was deteriorating.
Furthermore, because of its location near the Coke Works
the camp residents were confronted by a number of very
unpleasant environmental conditions. Whenever the wind
blew from one particular direction, it carried gasses from
the coke battery; whenever the wind blew from the opposite
direction, it brought fumes from the tar pits. Thus,
people often experienced unpleasant, if not noxious odors,
and women found that their laundry soon became sooted if
hung out to dry. Moreover, one Bethlehem Steel executive
offered the health factor as explanation for the eventual
closing of the Labor Camp.

About 1935 the Corporation constructed a meeting
hall at the Camp. This structure provided all residents
with a site for a kindergarten, dance hall, Mexican cinema,
Sunday school, and meeting place for the Boy Scouts
(Minority Life 1963:3-4). In fact, it was in this hall
that twenty Mexicans met in order to organize La Sociedad
Azteca Mexicana in 1937, holding meetings there gratis
until the camp closed in 1939.

Mexican Americans who lived in the Labor Camp as
children frequently recall its physical layout with greater
clarity and detail than do persons who resided there only
during their adult years. Invariably those who were boys
in the camp praise the nearby open countryside which served
as a playground well-suited for active youths. This
expanse included a creek, where in one location swam boys
and men, nude, while in another swam girls and women,
modestly attired in dresses. This creek provided some
people with fishing, and the older boys an opportunity so
sail the crude boats and rafts which they built (Ibid.:4).
However, informants agree that those using the swimming

hole faced the possibility of being butted by a heifer
which had been specially trained to do so by the farmer who
owned land adjoining the creek. For adventurous youngsters
the farms, fields, and woods behind the camp offered ample
opportunity for exploration and adventure.

Idealized Views of the Camp

Although the following statements made by informants
are presented in rather brief form, this brevity should not
be taken as evidence that Mexicans only rarely idealize
while reminiscing about camp life. Rather, it is because
of the redundancy of informants who praise the camp that
little need be written here.

A certain informant credits the Bethlehem Steel
Corporation with "providing homes, free light, free coke
for heat, some furniture for family use, and land for
garden use and the raising of chickens, ducks, pigs, geese,
and the like." In fact, to this man as well as to other
Mexicans, the camp constituted a "paradise" in contrast
with the living conditions which they had experienced prior
to migration from Mexico (Ibid.:2-3).

Another informant, one who had lived in the Labor
Camp as a child, praises the general reciprocity which
characterized camp life. He recalls that everyone in the
camp was poor; moreover he also reports that people
regularly shared their possessions and assisted one
another. When one woman had to go into town, a neighbor
would suckle her hungry infant. The slaughtering of a hog
raised in someone's backyard usually occasioned gifts of
meat to many of the other families. Informants also claim
that many residents were connected by the fictive kinship
bonds of compadrazgo (co-godparenthood). The words of one
informant express a prevalent sentiment: "There was
always someone to lend a helping hand whether it was a
Mexican family, a Hungarian family, or any other family."
Other informants stress that "it was just like one big
family." Thus, to these informants the familial atmosphere
in the Labor Camp far outweighed any problems of poverty.
In analysis one notes that these modes of customary
assistance also constitute effective adaptations to poverty.
Furthermore, one might observe that this perception of life

in the Labor Camp closely resembles the attitude about the Indian reservation as a community which has been held by many members of the Pan-Indian movement. According to Hertzberg they believe that "The Indian community had a remarkable potential for social health and satisfaction for its members" (1971:315). Viewed in this manner former residents of either the Labor Camp or an Indian reservation could indeed recall past years with great nostalgia.

One Informant's Stark Description

A Mexican American who lived in the Labor Camp as a child recalls his youth in vivid terms. He describes each house as being:

> A wooden frame block with six square rooms--one electric cord hanging from each ceiling, one outside toilet, one coke bin and slag stones for a lawn. It seems my pop was always patching up the exhaust pipes on the coke stove and the coke heater in the parlor. Mom was always scrubbing and spraying and pouring lime in the toilet. The Company gave us the coke, wood and lime and they also gave as a 'magic' book--it was like money, we could buy anything on it. On Saturdays they would let us take a shower in the dispensary.
>
> We had a desire to become not only proficient but champions at all the local activities. We became

excellent soccer players (later we supplied the
High School all it's teams--16 successive years as
District 11 champions); we became very good at
baseball and swimming. I'll never forget that
polluted stream that ran thru the Company's coke
plant with its muddy banks and magically colored
streams of Coke gas floating on its surface.

We always knew when winter was approaching for
the Company would park a train atop the slag
banks that overshadowed our village and they
would dump several carloads of used lumber over
the bank sides. Then the whole village would
bustle--fathers, mothers, daughters and sons--
age was no barrier--everyone helping to drag the
lumber home to stack the cellar for the coming
winter. It was funny, everyone trying to get the
choice pieces, sometimes fights would break out.
You would see whole families pitted against one
another and the winners would then take the choice
pieces. Here and there you would see someone
hobbling home and we knew at a glance that they
had stepped on a rusty nail--this was common,
because we were mostly barefoot or wore a very
cheap sneaker.

Then, when the wood was cleaned up, the Company
would dump a couple of carloads of Coke and the
whole village would turn out again. The entire
household could be seen converging on the coke
pile carrying burlap bags, buckets (25 lb. lard
cans), homemade wheelbarrows, wagons, and pop
would carry the homemade shovel. We would fill
our containers, and when we were all loaded up we
would start the procession home to the coal bin in
the cellar. Pop would pull the homemade wagon
with the high sides and iron wheels and I would
push at the back--mom would carry two buckets, one
in each hand. Following mom were my two older
sisters, each with a burlap bag of coke strung

over their shoulders and bringing up the rear was
my little brother carrying the homemade shovel,
God forbid what might have happened to our shovel
should we have left it unattended even for the
briefest moment. We would repeat these trips back
to the coke pile till late at night, sometimes for
days at a time until pop felt there was enough
wood and coke in the bins for the winter--then we
would sit back and wait for those long, cold and
bitter winters to swoop down on our rickety houses.

I could not help but wonder as we walked back to
the coke pile, I would pause and look up at the
people (it seemed like hundreds of them), bent over
and filling their containers and then I would look
over my shoulder toward the main road and watch
the 'gringo's' drive by in their shiny cars and I
used to wonder what they thought of us--what a
picture we must have painted for them!

As the long winter would set in on us, we would
spend the long hours gathering round the kitchen
table and mom and pop would teach us how to read
and speak Spanish, my older sisters would teach
us all what little English they had learned that
day in school, they were both in the elementary
school now. Oh, how I yearned for the coming year
when I would start school, I was almost 7 now.
Mom thought I was just a little too small to walk
three miles to the first grade--but oh how I
yearned to go. Pop thought it unwise because I
knew no English, but surely I thought there must
be someone in that school who could help me get
started, oh well, too late to start this year,
perhaps next.

As the hour grew late, mom would whip up a batch
of hot cocoa Mexican style--this was hot (warm)
and rich, really delicious and invigorating, then
we would take turns at washing behind the ears and

brushing the teeth. As mom would tuck us in for
the night, pop would stock the kitchen stove and
the parlor heater hoping that they would burn
evenly thru the cold night. This always made it
uncomfortable for a while for the added coke
would give off new gasses for a few moments but
then the odor would go away and we would snuggle
in bed to await our prayer session which was
always led by mom.

In the wintertime we used two bedrooms, the two
that were exposed to the parlor heater, mom and
pop in the one and the two boys and two girls
shared the other, separate beds, of course, mom
was fussy about that! Mom would turn all the
lights out and then she would kneel between our
beds and lead us through our prayers in Spanish.
Mom was so complete, so kind and good to all of
us. Then we would lay there and watch the shadows
of the flames in the parlor heater dance across
walls and ceilings in the parlor. Speaking was
forbidden after the prayers, so we were left to
our own imagination and as I watched the shadows
on the ceiling, I could see goblins and ugly faces
and just as quickly they would turn to shapes of
funny faces such as clowns, at times I could see
cowboys chasing Indians and then I would see
people dancing and fiddlers playing.[16]

Solidarity vs. Disunity

Without doubt, the most salient characteristic of
life at the Labor Camp which informants today remember
nostalgically is the group solidarity and mutual cooperation
of the residents. Existence there seems to have preserved

[16]This account, written by a second-generation
Mexican American, consists of portions of a letter--now a
part of the Pennsylvania State Labor Archives--which he
wrote to a labor historian. The description is reproduced
herein with the permission of its author.

more aspects of the folk community than one might have
expected to find within the industrial complex of the
nation's second largest steel producer. It might be
suggested that the Mexicans, very far away indeed from
kinsmen and natal villages, sought to preserve or to
recreate former patterns of social relationships with their
new neighbors in "El Campo," despite the ethnic diversity
of the residents. On the other hand, if in actuality some
Mexicans had migrated from closed corporate peasant
communities, then the formation of close social ties based
more upon residence than upon kinship should not be
surprising.

Some of the adaptations made by camp dwellers to
life in Bethlehem can together be considered as evidence
for organic solidarity. For example, several persons
capitalized on their nucleated residence pattern by offering goods and services desired by fellow residents and
countrymen. The petit entrepreneurs of the Labor Camp did
not restrict themselves to gardening and the raising of a
few animals or poultry. For example, one man served as a

camp barber, working at this trade after finishing his
shift at the Coke Works. During prohibition, another ran
a "speak-easy" in his house. One enterprising Mexican
youth bought moonshine for $2.00 per gallon, rebottling
it into pints and half-pints to sell for a total of either
$4.00 or $5.00 per gallon. A Slavic housewife in the camp
practiced midwifery, reportedly having delivered between
thirty and forty Mexican American children. Several
Mexicans joined together with a few Spanish and Portuguese
men, forming a small orchestra in order to provide music
for dances. Thus, oftentimes disregarding differences in
ethnicity, a number of the camp dwellers provided their
co-residents with several specialized services.

Apparently the camp dwellers quite frequently held
celebrations. The Virgin of Guadalupe, the patron saint
of Mexico, was honored on December 12; Mexican independence,
on September 16; and the defeat of the French at Puebla, on
May 5. People generally commemorated their saint's name
days rather than their own birthdays. Invariably every
other week the Mexicans drank--whiskey and tequila were

133

preferred--and sang far into the night following the
biweekly payday. Indeed, an Anglo informant who worked
with Mexicans in the neighboring Coke Works recalls that
sometimes when on the night shift, he and others would be
able to sneak off to a party in the camp--"having a good
time" while still remaining on company premises. Based upon
these visits he praises the Mexicans' generousity while
warmly describing their celebrations. Funerals also were
major social events; the accompanying wakes lasting two or
three days. Usually the deceased was placed in the front
room of his house for "viewing," while Mexican dishes were
served in a back room of the house. Whether for festivities
or mourning, such social occasions did contribute to the
group solidarity which past residents of the camp now
fondly recall.

        Nevertheless, despite the fact that many informants
continue to emphasize the harmony and eunomia of existence
in the Labor Camp, still others assert that Camp residents
also experienced conflicts with one another. For example,
Vallarta, a married informant whose wife had remained in

Mexico, was living in the camp in a consensual union.
During the depression, because of the scarcity of work, he
was forced to accept "relief" funds in order to support
his household. In contrast, his neighbor was a relatively
prosperous man who continued in steady employment. So
great was the outrage and moral indignation of this neighbor's wife that she began to taunt Vallarta's "wife,"
making faces at her and even throwing dish water at her.
Vallarta was forced to solve his problem by promising a
severe beating to the neighbor if his wife did not cease
her harrassment. Furthermore, Vallarta implied that these
sanctions resulted more from his consensual union than from
his having accepted "relief."

Other informants recount that there was a fight in
the Labor Camp approximately once each week. In addition,
it is said that one man was killed for having an affair
with another man's wife. Indeed, to some Mexicans, the
violence which occurred in the Labor Camp befitted the
sensational accounts about Mexicans which had been published
in local newspapers. Nevertheless, until the steel company

closed the Labor Camp in 1939, this residential area permitted Mexicans to maintain a social solidarity which may still recall nostalgically in 1970.[17]

---

[17]According to some informants the Corporation had been gradually phasing out the Labor Camp for several years prior to 1939. That is, each time a family moved out of the camp the vacated house was demolished. Several informants have priased the Bethlehem Steel Corporation for the policies which it utilized in the closing of the Labor Camp, while at the same time regretting that they were forced to leave. The company permitted camp residents to salvage building materials from their houses and a number of Mexicans utilized this lumber to begin constructing new homes for themselves. On the one hand, the executives of the Bethlehem Steel Corporation finally may have realized that, unless otherwise persuaded, many of the camp's residents would remain there indefinitely. In fact, several informants completely agree with this surmise, saying that they would still be living in the Labor Camp if they had been permitted to do so. On the other hand, the need for defense security geared to war production in the steel plants has been offered by one executive of the Bethlehem Steel Corporation as the reason why the Company closed the Labor Camp; it is said that the Corporation legally could not have restricted those who wished to visit camp residents (who were actually residing within the perimeter of the steel plant) solely to those persons with security clearances. One wonders whether the operation of the coke ovens involved any secret knowledge vital to the national defense. Nevertheless, the Company may have desired to more "efficiently" utilize the land upon which the Labor Camp was located, having anticipated a vastly increased demand for steel production. Whether or not the Corporation actually closed the Labor Camp for these particular reasons, it is undeniable that in 1939 many Mexicans were forced to move from the camp, leaving behind the group solidarity and familial atmosphere which had characterized their life in El Campo.

Mexican Voluntary Associations
in Bethlehem

Because of their inter-cultural rural-urban migration, one expects Mexicans to have organized voluntary associations after settling in Bethlehem during the 1920's. As observed elsewhere (Chapter I), fundamentally changed situations, whether social, cultural, economic, or political, stimulate persons to form and participate in voluntary associations. Many of the Mexicans who founded Bethlehem's colonia mexicana were semi-literate peasants who had no previous exposure to an urban milieu. The culture shock resulting from their contact with the technology of steel production caused some to flee at "eighty miles an hour" (Taylor 1931b:ix). Indeed, the Mexicans migrated from one society into another society, entirely foreign. The extensive changes experienced by Mexicans as a result of their migration and subsequent residence in Bethlehem lead to the expectation that voluntary associations should have been organized by them in Pennsulvania, serving as mechanisms for adaptation to their new milieu.

The economic conditions in Bethlehem which at that time confronted the Mexicans further indicate a need for Mexican voluntary associations which would promote improvement in these conditions. Fully employed unskilled steelworkers received wages at little above the poverty level. The frequency of under-employment and irregular employment caused major uncertainties for steelworkers who needed to feed and clothe their families. Furthermore, loss of wages because of illness was an everpresent possibility. These factors effectively preclude the amassing of sizeable savings; therefore Mexicans needed financial aid from others.

In 1926, for example, one informant arrived in Bethlehem, completely destitute, and was hired by the steel corporation; however he was faced with the prospect of subsisting without funds in the corporation's Labor Camp for the two weeks until he received his first pay check. He was fortunate, nevertheless, because another camp resident from the same village in Jalisco fed him and even took him to a motion picture show. Given the fact

that some Mexicans originated in almost every state of
northern and central Mexico, rarely could Mexicans laboring
in the United States depend upon assistance through a
complex network of consanguineal, affinal, and fictive
kinship bonds; dyadic contracts; or other traditional
social relationships involving reciprocal obligations
(Foster 1961:1173-1o92; Mintz and Wolf 1950:341). Because
Mexicans emigrated as individuals, rather than in groups
from the same village, Mexicans residing in the United
States thus needed to develop some alternative means of
mutual assistance. In other words, in Bethlehem there was
a need for group-wide integrative institutions which could
supplant the traditional bases of localized reciprocity.
One might note, too, that the emergence of beneficial
associations, which are found wherever Mexicans have
settled in the United States, can be interpreted as partial
replacements for the reciprocal ties which are found in
Mexican villages. For Mexicans who resided in Bethlehem,
illness could have a devastating financial impact upon
them because they were already impoverished. Therefore,

voluntary associations which guarantee payments to the
sick provide important, if not also necessary, adjustments
to residence in Bethlehem.

At least three beneficial associations have been
organized by Bethlehem's small population of Mexicans. In
1927, residents of the colonia mexicana organized the
short-lived Union Protectora which was later disbanded
because of the doubly mistaken belief that aliens could not
legally organize a union (in reality the Unión Protectora
was a beneficial association, not a labor union; the term
for "labor union" in Spanish is sindicato rather than
unión; furthermore, aliens were not legally precluded from
organizing labor unions) (Taylor 1931b:17-18). Without
doubt, given the adamant opposition of steel company
executives to any unionization of steelworkers, these
corporation officials would not have encouraged the continuation of any voluntary association which appeared to
English speakers to be a labor union. With respect to
dues and benefits, the voluntary association which the
Mexicans organized in the following year was rather similar

to the contemporary Sociedad Azteca Mexicana. By 1930,
130 members had each paid a fifty cent initiation fee and
$1.00 per month in dues; in return they were eligible to
receive sick benefits of $3.00 per week, for a maximum of
thirteen weeks, with benefits commencing after three weeks
of illness. Upon the death of a member, the association
paid a death benefit of $100 to his survivors in addition
to the proceeds of a collection of $1.00 per capita of
membership. But upon the death of a Mexican who did not
belong to the association, a voluntary collection was taken
among members of the colonia; because many Mexicans read
La Prensa of San Antonio, which could be purchased locally,
the list of donors was usually published in that Spanish
language newspaper.[18]

---

[18] As the major Spanish language daily newspaper
which served Mexican Americans, La Prensa's circulation
extended far beyond the borders of Texas. Because of the
newspaper's wide circulation, new items were published
which related to colonias as far away as Bethlehem. Public
acknowledgment of death and the mourners participation
in funerals seems common. One informant produced a photograph of the persons attending such a rite in 1929. It
shows nearly fifty persons. The informant's explanation
for the placement of mourners around the open, elvated
coffin is that in this way the mother of the deceased
would be convinced of her son's death. Furthermore, she
would recognize at least sixteen of the witnesses as
hailing from her village of San Jose Tateposco, Jalisco.

Perhaps the implementation of the association's motto, _Por el bien colectivo_ (for the collective good), foreshadowed the end of the association: penniless Mexicans who arrived in Bethlehem were given loans without incurring to themselves any legal obligation of repayment. While speaking in a guarded manner, one elderly informant stated that the members disbanded because of the Great Depression after having divided the contents of the treasury among themselves. However, other, seemingly more candid, informants blamed the disbandment upon a treasurer who had absconded with the funds. Obviously, he had valued his own good above the collective good. A later result of this development, however, may have been a heightening of skepticism and suspicion on the part of the members of the _Sociedad Azteca Mexicana_ which was organized in 1937.

Because of the absence of formally organized, non-religious, beneficial voluntary associations in rural areas of Mexico's _Mesa Central_, Mexicans clearly did not emigrate from Mexico with plans for organizing such associations. Despite the fact that the majority of the

Mexicans who migrated to Bethlehem had resided for no more than one year elsewhere in the United States, this duration was surely sufficient for them to discover advantages of the voluntary associations which Mexicans maintained in other cities.

Mexicans were further stimulated to organize voluntary associations by virtue of their residence in a "nation of joiners." Moreover, the examples of numerous local populations of immigrants which had already founded ethnic associations similarly encourage them to form their own associations. Such was indeed the case in Bethlehem, Pennsylvania.

The absence of a formally organized Mexican association in Bethlehem throughout most of the years of the Great Depression presents something of a paradox. During the several preceding years, when jobs and money had been more plentiful, there had been a succession of two short-lived Mexican mutual benefit associations; however from 1930 until 1937 no Mexican organization assured monetary assistance in time of illness or bereavement. On

the one hand, an "old timer" explains the hiatus by saying
that Mexicans could ill-afford the association's dues. On
the other hand, most Mexicans never had greater need for
the sickness and death benefits than they did during this
period of widespread unemployment and severe underemployment.

After 1930 some assistance was, nevertheless,
forthcoming through the efforts of Father Cordova, the
pastor who had been instrumental in the formation of the
Ibero-American Congregation of Holy Infancy Roman Catholic
Church, and many Mexicans did belong to this church's
voluntary associations. However, the aid which was provided mainly consisted of an occasional food basket for
needy Mexican families and distribution at Christmas of
gifts which had been donated to Father Cordova. By far,
the greatest social benefit which was derived from the
existence of this congregation appears to have been an
increase in solidarity both within and among the Mexican,
Spanish, and Portuguese populations.

Although there is a hiatus of seven years during
which a non-religious Mexican voluntary association was

lacking, shared attendance at Holy Infancy Roman Catholic
Church kept Mexicans and other Latins in contact with one
another despite residence in different sections of
Bethlehem's south side. Without doubt, when the Mexican
Aztec Society was finally organized it was not simply a
matter of chance that a few Portuguese and Spaniards also
became charter members.

Despite the disbandment in 1930 of the Mexican
mutual benefit association, members of the colonia mexicana
formed temporary associations for the purpose of organizing
dances and other social events including ones in commemoration for Mexican national holidays. Also, it should be
recalled that several Mexicans and a few other camp
residents organized an informal dance band which provided
music for their social gatherings. These and other informal,
if not also temporary, voluntary associations did continue
actively throughout the depression years. Therefore, one
may consider Mexican voluntarism during the period 1930
through 1937 as an instance of Tsouderos's first stage in
the formalization of a voluntary association--a stage

characterized by informal voluntary associations (Chapman
and Tsouderos 1955:308).

In a superficial analysis one might point out the
inconsistency between the assertion that voluntary
associations are adaptive for rural-urban migrants and the
later observation that the Mexicans disbanded their mutual
benefit associations after a total of less than four years
of association activity. However, one can present a case
that this response is entirely consistent with both Mexican
culture and the changed economic conditions in Bethlehem.
In the first place, steelworkers and other laborers rarely
knew how many days they would be permitted to work during
each subsequent week. With a measure of eloquence, an old
Spaniard, who has lived for many years in Bethlehem,
describes the Great Depression as being "cuando los frijoles
estaban tan altos que no podían alcanzar" (When the beans
were so high that one could not reach them). Furthermore,
as during many periods of severe economic depression those
industrial workers who lacked accumulated resources

inevitably encountered economic uncertainties which
resembled the adversities which Mexican peasants have
survived.

In rural Mexico, as in many peasant societies, the
time-honored adaptation to uncertainties within an unpro-
ductive environment has been retrenchment within one's
community, resorting to subsistence agriculture with some
additional security provided by a network of mutual obligations. In Bethlehem the poorest Mexicans (those residing
in the Labor Camp) adapted to the Great Depression in ways
functionally analogous to the strategies often employed by
agrarian Mexicans. Encouraged by the Bethlehem Steel
Corporation, camp dwellers to some extent subsisted
through their own efforts at gardening and animal husbandry,
even though they were residing on the grounds of an
industrial complex. Despite conflict among camp dwellers,
the Mexicans greatly complemented their subsistence
activities with dependence upon mutual assistance based
upon kinship, compadrazgo, and common residence. In other
words, although continued voluntarism could have been

adaptive for Mexicans at this time, their residence in the
camp permitted a much more direct solution to the problems
caused by economic depression: production of "beans" in
subsistence plots and dependence upon localized reciprocity
patterns with others sharing similar economic conditions.
In light of these reapplications of traditional Mexican
coping mechanisms, non-Mexican informants who refer to the
Labor Camp as the "Mexican village" may have isolated the
functions which the camp actually served at that time.

Assuming that the hypothesis is correct that
Mexicans' adaptations to the Great Depression were effected
via a "return to the village," either through physical
repatriation or simulation of village economic and social
patterns, then the formation of the Mexican Aztec Society
early in 1937 constitutes evidence for renewed willingness
on the part of Mexicans to reject traditional coping
methods in favor of mutual assistance achieved through
formal voluntarism. Indeed, over fifty percent of the
association's charter members did reside in the Labor
Camp. However, as stated in the association's minutes, the

Mexicans formed this association in direct response to the
economic upturn of 1936 and 1937 rather choosing this
particular time by pure chance. The optimism which was
generated by this economic progress also encouraged
Mexicans to once again experiment with a mode of cooperation (the formally organized mutual benefit voluntary
association) which, although not found in their natal
villages, had been advantageously utilized by members of
many other ethnic groups residing in Bethlehem. Formation
of the Mexican Aztec Society constitutes a substitution of
a "modern" coping mechanism for other mechanisms traditional
to Mexican culture. This interpretation in addition to
earlier discussion of possible excessive reliance by
anthropologists upon the notion of "traditional" Mexican or
Mexican American culture (vide Chapter I) suggests that one
should not make the a priori assumption that the Mexican
Aztec Society does, indeed, serve as a bastion of traditional
Mexican culture. As will be seen in subsequent chapters,
to some extent this voluntary association has also contributed to the assimilation of Mexican Americans in Bethlehem,
Pennsylvania.

CHAPTER III

FORMALIZATION OF THE MEXICAN AZTEC
SOCIETY: 1937 TO 1970[1]

Preliminary Remarks

In the words of John Tsouderos formalization consists of "the process by which groups follow prescribed patterns of procedure; an increasing complexity in the social structure, a progressive prescription and standardization of social relationships and finally, an increasing bureaucratization of the organization" (Chapin and Tsouderos 1955:306). In other words the concept of formalization denotes all of the various processes which collectively cause the transformation of a once informal voluntary association into a formal and bureaucratic voluntary association. However, Tsouderos's model of the formalization process focuses more upon the consequences of

---

[1] I have been able to provide a detailed diachronic treatment of the Mexican Aztec Society only because I have been generously granted access to the association's minute books and other records.

For the purpose of brevity this voluntary association, which in its history has been called by several names, shall be referred to herein as "the Azteca," an appellation often used by the members.

formalization than upon processes which generate the
observed temporal patterns. Nevertheless, utilization of
this construct as an heuristic framework facilitates
description of the Mexican Aztec Society's history while
also testing the validity of the Tsouderos model. If
Tsouderos's formalization model does accurately describe
the temporal patterns exhibited by the Mexican Aztec
Society, the members of this association must have formu-
lated explicit procedures for maintenance of the association, developed group norms which result in increasingly
standardized behavior of members, instituted an increasingly differentiated set of membership statuses and roles,
and eventually also produced a bureaucratic organization.
At least in broad outline the Mexican Aztec Society does
appear to have exhibited formalization; however Tsouderos's
more detailed statements about formalization must be tested
against the history of this voluntary association before
any conclusive evaluation can be made of the utility of
this construct.

Stages of Formalization

Stage 1

Tsouderos's first stage of formalization, the period
characterized by informal voluntary associations, corresponds to the several years in the Mexican colonia's history
during which no formal associations existed--more
specifically 1930 through 1937 (Chapin and Tsouderos 1955:
308). During this early period of the Great Depression
Mexicans did form informal voluntary associations for the
purpose of organizing celebrations of Mexican patriotic
holidays. These festivities served both symbolic and
sociability functions. Not until 1937 did the Mexicans
found an enduring voluntary association and explicitly
enumerate by-laws which were to govern their organization.
Among other results, the charter members of the Mexican
Aztec Society formalized previously existing, although
informal, bonds of shared interest. Therefore, rather
than constituting a complete departure from preceding
events the creation of the Mexican Aztec Society may more

accurately be considered as a formalization of previously
informal modes of association.

According to Tsouderos, voluntary associations in
the second stage have instituted both an election process
and one or more formal leadership statuses (Ibid.).
Indeed, with the inception of the Mexican Aztec Society
in 1937 Bethlehem's colonia mexicana entered into the
second stage in the formalization of their voluntarism.

Stage 2

Formation

In 1937, when the United States economy showed
some signs of recovering from the Great Depression, Arturo
Jimenez and one other Mexican decided that their colonia
should no longer lack its own mutual benefit association.
Accordingly, in order to promote the idea of a Mexican
association, these organizers personally visited many
Mexican families prior to February 21, 1937, on which date
an organizational meeting was held in the Coke Works Room
(a meeting or assembly hall) on the premises of the

Bethlehem Steel Corporation's Labor Camp.[2] Before adjourn-
ing this initial session the persons present chose to name
their association Sociedad Centro Cultural y Benéfica
(Beneficial Society and Cultural Center).

Considering that a total of twenty members
attended the second meeting, one may infer that the Mexicans
responded enthusiastically to the idea of their own voluntary association; in fact, when compared with the attendance
at meetings during subsequent years, usually one-fifth or
less of the active membership, the attendance of twenty

---

[2]In that year the association was called, in turn,
Sociedad Centro Cultural Mexicano (Mexican Cultural Center
Society), Centro Cultural y Beneficio Mexicano (Mexican
Cultural and Beneficial Center), Sociedad Benefica Mexicano
de Ambos Sexos (American Mexican Beneficial Society of
Both Sexes); and in 1941 Sociedad Azteca Mexicana de Ambos
Sexos (Mexican Aztec Society of Both Sexes). The motto of
this association has always been, however, Unión y
Fraternidad (Unity and Fraternity).
    Members collective feelings of vulnerability are
demonstrated by events occurring in October of 1937. They
became alarmed upon being informed that one of their
number--a non-Mexican woman--was initiating a legal suit
against the association. Because no one understood the
basis for her action the association's president appointed
a committee to interview her in order to ascertain her
reason, and, if possible, to dissuade her from continuing
the suit. Investigation revealed that the woman had indeed
written a letter to the association, but that for lack of
knowledge of Spanish she had written in English; when a
friend translated the letter into Spanish the request for
sick benefits, the reason for drafting the letter, inad-
vertently became converted into a threat to sue the
association.

persons is unusually large. It should be noted that
attendance at meetings, although required by the by-laws,
is not necessary for the receipt of benefits. (Not until
December of 1937 did as many as thirty-three persons join
the association. Therefore, for that year an average
attendance of twenty members constitutes compelling
evidence of a high motivation of members.)[3] Furthermore,
only in unusual circumstances does active participation in
any voluntary association--especially an instrumental
association--greatly exceed twenty percent. What is even
more remarkable, however, is that the members sustained
such an active interest in their new association that they
held a total of twenty meetings during the ten months which

---

[3]Taking the number of voting ("active" rather than
"social") members of the association as approximately one
hundred and considering that no more than five hundred
Mexican Americans could be eligible for active membership,
this means that at least twenty percent of the adult
Mexican Americans in Bethlehem belong to the Mexican Aztec
Society as active members. This does not include in the
calculations additional Mexican Americans who are only
social members. Despite the small number of Mexican
Americans who choose to be active members, David Sills
judges from numerous studies of urban American populations
that less than twenty percent of all urban dwellers actively
participate in at least one voluntary association (1968:
365). Although these two statistics are not entirely
comparable, it should be apparent that Mexican American
participation in the Mexican Aztec Society is at least as
frequent as the participation in voluntary associations
observed for the urban population of the United States.

remained of 1937. Without doubt, this enthusiasm was
heightened by the prompt receipt of praise and encouragement from the Mexican Consul General in Philadelphia;
further, he promised to meet with the association's members
in the near future.

Status and Role

In order to qualify for membership in the Mexican
Aztec Society, one must reside in Bethlehem, Hellertown,
or Freemansburg, Pennsylvania and have attained an age of
at least fifteen years; however, Negroes are excluded from
membership.[4] Only by vote of the "general assembly"--
members in good standing who are in attendance at a meeting
of the Mexican Aztec Society--can an applicant be formally
accepted or rejected, as a member. Following an initial
probationary period of three months, new members then
qualify for full benefits as "active" members provided
that they regularly pay their dues of $.75 per month and

---

[4]In 1953 members of the Mexican Aztec Society voted
to delete the discriminatory clause and to raise the minimum
age of applicants to twenty-one. The former was required as
a precondition to incorporation and the latter was required
by the Liquor Control Board of the Commonwealth of Pennsylvania.
    Reflecting the residential dispersion of Mexican
Americans during the past score of years, beginning in 1953
applicants qualified for membership by residing anywhere
within a twenty-five mile radius of Bethlehem.

avoid all "improper conduct" (see Chapter IV). However, the requirement of mandatory attendance at all meetings has not proved enforceable. Furthermore, all members are required to attend the funerals of deceased members; they must attend all meetings "in full control of their mental faculties" (Chapter IV); and they must work without financial compensation as officer, committee member, or in any other capacity deemed "for the good of the society."

The official leadership statuses of the association consist of president, vice-president, secretary, assistant secretary, treasurer, vocales (2), and commissioner.[5] With the exception of commissioner these officials comprise the "board of directors" all of whom must be members in good standing who are literate in Spanish and either Mexican or the Spanish spouse of a Mexican.[6] The association's by-laws also include details describing the procedure by which officers are to be nominated and elected. In this association the roles of president, vice-president,

[5] Vocal translates as "member of a governing body" (Cuyas 1966:568), but in this particular context "substitute" would better identify the leadership status of vocal.

[6] By 1953 the by-laws had been reworded in order to permit Mexican Americans, in addition to Mexicans, to hold office. However, although enforcement has been ignored for several years, the requirement that officers be literate in Spanish was not deleted.

secretary, assistant secretary and treasurer follow common usage; however, the two vocals are required to substitute for any absent officer. The commissioner—sometimes referred to as "scrutinizer" by members—is entrusted with the verification of all association records whether associated with officers or the various committees. In these respects members did indeed formalize their association's social structure.

In addition to ad hoc committees, formed to meet various special needs, the president annually appointed an electoral committee, a committee for festivities, a house committee, a committee of public health, and a collection committee. The committee for festivities, which might have been termed the social committee, organized dances and other social affairs; the house committee served in a janitorial capacity. However, the committee of public health was encharged with establishing the eligibility for benefits of all sick members. Lastly, each of the collectors was responsible for collecting dues from members residing in one of the following locations: the Coke

Works area, Northampton Heights, or the city of Bethlehem.[7]
For most purposes the members of the Mexican Aztec Society
had delineated the structure of their voluntary association
during its first year of existence. Furthermore, as a
consequence of these formalizations leadership expectations
became incorporated into various social statuses which
endure beyond the performances of particular elective
officials. In other words, person and associational
leadership status have become differentiated.

From its inception the association often depended
upon committees (comiciones) encharged with the resolution
of any problems or issues upon which the general assembly
had become dead-locked. Although not an unusual parliamentary procedure, the practice of frequent and continuing decision-making on the part of the officers and a small
nucleus of appointed committee members pre-empted the
perogatives of the assembly; this oligarchical pattern

---

[7]The collectors and the commissioners of public
health apparently reflect members' cognitive categorizations
of the areas which they themselves inhabited. Collectors
and Public Health Commissioners were appointed for the Coke
Works area (variously rendered as 'Kok,' "Cok,' 'La Cocoa'),
'the Heights' (Northampton Heights, a borough), and 'the
town' (Bethlehem's South Side). One notes that the designa-
tion of one collector for each of the areas was once
adequate, for few Mexicans lived in other locations within
the region of Bethlehem.

intensified over the years. One notes that although members do learn formal democratic procedures, this does not necessarily imply the complete implementation of democracy. Furthermore, because sociologist David Sills (1968:369) presented considerable evidence in support of the notion that voluntary associations are inherently characterized by minority rule, one should not single out the Mexican Aztec Society as an unusually undemocratic organization.

Despite incomplete empirical adherence to official Mexican Aztec Society by-laws, the members had, nevertheless, enacted a set of rules which far surpassed the requirement that associations in the second stage of formalization must have instituted an election process and one or more leadership statuses.

Tsouderos predicts that if a voluntary association at Stage 1 becomes yet more formalized the members will have further differentiated their leadership statuses and may additionally have created at least one occupational status. Rather than striving for formalization per se, members struggled to transform their association into an

organization which would augment their social prestige
while maintaining the organization's mutual assistance
function and more fully providing for sociability. The
Mexicans chose to realize their goals by legally incor-
porating their association, renting or purchasing permanent
quarters, and obtaining a liquor license. Members perceived that by means of these accomplishments they could
provide themselves with a setting in which Mexicans could
drink and generally interact with fellow countrymen. Not
of least importance was the pride which members felt at
being able to invite non-Mexicans to "our club." However,
the Mexican Aztec Society became increasingly formalized
as a consequence of these cherished goals rather than
because of a desire for formalization.

Increased Formalization

The Mexicans quickly became aware that certain
activities of their voluntary association were regulated
by various laws. It was during 1939 that the association's
officers first inquired into the legality of selling beer in
the meeting room; it was probably also at that time that the

association's members first discovered that acquisition of
the right to sell alcoholic beverages was far from simple.
Members' initial concern over the association's legality
eventually became transmuted into a desire for a state
charter (incorporation) and a liquor license. Protracted
discussions of these topics appear repeatedly in the
minutes until 1954 when both are finally obtained. During
the intervening years payment of costly legal fees
constituted an unsurmountable obstacle, but the major
impediment to obtaining a charter and license, however,
lay in the members' incomplete and inaccurate knowledge of
the steps to be followed in this detailed process. Members'
confusion about names legally permissable for incorporated
associations repeatedly led them to modify that of their
"club." Notably, in 1939, the association voted to prefix
the word "American" to its name in an effort to expedite
incorporation. For many years, however, these efforts were
to be without success.

Even in the 1940's the Azteca members continued to
harbor some of the same fears which pervaded their colonia

mexicana during the 1920's. At that time twenty years earlier the Mexicans had disbanded a voluntary association because of the mistaken belief that their organization was illegal. During the 1940's these Mexican immigrants reasoned that because their association was not incorporated, its existence violated the laws of the nation in which they then resided. Indeed, members' fears were so intense that they expressed concern about "police dissolving our meeting or even arresting us without being able to appeal to any legal procedure." Although the members seldom expressed their fears concerning the association's legality in such vivid language, apprehensions about this subject were stated in the minutes of meetings during every year from 1940 through 1943. In order to achieve their goal the association's officers took steps to (1) translate their regulations into English, (2) compile the names and addresses of all members, and (3) provide to the appropriate state officials the names and addresses of both the founding and present officers. Further, upon the advice of legal counsel, the association deleted the word "beneficial" from

its name, thus becoming the <u>Sociedad</u> <u>Azteca</u> <u>Mexicana</u> <u>de</u>
<u>Ambos</u> <u>Sexos</u> (Mexican Aztec Society of Both Sexes). Concern
for legal status persisted, however, in 1946, for example,
the members decided that when the club facilities were
located in a permanent hall "the char [charter] will be
more easily obtained." At last some of these efforts on
the part of association members to acquire formal legal
recognition were effective: on December 23, 1953 the
Commonwealth of Pennsylvania granted the Mexican Aztec
Society of Both Sexes the legal recognition for which the
members had striven during more than sixteen years.

At about the same time, when aliens were being
encouraged to become naturalized citizens of the United
States, members were told that in order for this beneficial
association to incorporate as a non-profit organization it
was necessary that each association officer be a citizen
of the United States. This requirement presented some
difficulty for the association, considering that all but
one of the officers were Mexican citizens and that only six
United States citizens could be found among the ranks of

the members. The assembly coped with this problem by
electing a dummy slate of officers who performed their
functions in title only; however for lack of eligible
members no one could be elected as second vocal.[8]

Not until October 1, 1952 did Mexican Aztec Society
members complete their long search for quarters by trans-
ferring association activities to a permanent (rented)
hall centrally located on the south side. At a special
session called to acknowledge the significance of the
occasion the president traced the location of meetings
"from the provisional hall at the no-longer existing Coke
Works Camp, the temporarily rented hall on the corner of
Second and Bessemer Streets, in the 'Heights' at the homes
of Mr. Jimenez and Mr. _____, as well as our many social
activities at the different halls of societies such as the
Ukranian Hall, the Portuguese Hall, the Italian Hall, etc.,
and now happily the opportune acquisition of the present
hall."

Several months after the Mexican Aztec Society had
received its charter, representatives of the Young Men's

_____

[8]One significant but indirect effect of this
adaptation is that the first second-generation Mexican
American to join the association, Juan Camacho, became an
elected official; in later years he became president of
the association.

Republican Club offered to sell their liquor license to the
Mexican association, an offer which was quickly accepted.
Because the number of liquor licenses in a given geographic
area is restricted by the Commonwealth of Pennsylvania
Liquor Control Board, often such a transaction is necessary
if a newly-chartered association is to maintain itself
financially: the sale of liquor in clubrooms is the
expected and usual means of self-support for the private
clubs of Pennsylvania.

Upon becoming licensed to sell liquor on the
premises the association began to resemble a commercial
night club. Of great import is the fact that association
members previously had had the responsibility of managing
only petit finances; almost overnight they became responsible for handling thousands of dollars of association
funds. Also, it was necessary to manage a sizeable
inventory and to remunerate several paid employees as well
as to keep the detailed records which the state Liquor
Control Board demanded. (The purchase of an adding machine
documents the increase in accounting problems.)

Because of the great expenditures in members' time
which the operation of a bar demanded, it was eventually
necessary to add the appointive status of steward to the
roster of officers; as manager of the bar the steward hired
and directed the bartenders. Almost immediately the
pecuniary aspects of association business concerning
voluntary labor, salaried labor, and raises began to demand
the greatest portion of the general assembly's attention.
Eventually, the general assembly voted to pay salaries to
almost every person working for the association. For
example, all members of the board of directors were granted
monthly expense accounts of $100 per officer. Also, in
1966 the general assembly alloted to the president an
additional expense account of $25 per month for the purpose
of entertaining guests.

The decision to institute the office of steward
constitutes some increased differentiation among the
association's leadership statuses. Moreover, at least
temporarily during the 1960's the association renumerated
the steward for full-time employment. However, the steward's

duties were limited to bartending and supervision of the clubhouse bar rather than the larger responsibilities of a professional executive in charge of all association matters. For these reasons the Mexican Aztec Society has only fleetingly, if ever, qualified for inclusion at the third stage of formalization.

Until 1954 active membership in this Mexican American association was open to all ethnic groups. The number of members grew so rapidly during that particular year with the result that Mexican Americans began to fear loss of control of their own voluntary association, especially to the incoming Puerto Ricans. Nevertheless, it was not until April of 1955 that the Mexican Aztec Society's members voted to accept social members, reserving "active" membership to only Mexican Americans and to their spouses.

For several years the members had wished to own their meeting rooms. After investigating and rejecting several other possibilities, in 1965 the Sociedad Azteca Mexicana tied its fortunes to the purchase of a large,

three story building.[9] On November 22, 1965 the general
assembly proudly held its first meeting in this newly
purchased hall. Converting the former furniture store
into association quarters, complete with kitchen and bar,
was accomplished through considerable contributions of
volunteer labor as well as large monetary expenditures.
It was not until May 7 that the members held their
association's "grand opening" which event also commemorated
the Mexican national holiday of May 5. This "gala" affair
included the performance of a hired Mexican orchestra,
Mariachis de Mexico, and the attendance of Mexican Americans
dressed in traditional attire.

Because members of the Mexican Aztec Society have
never organized a network of Mexican American voluntary
associations each of which recognize the authority of a
central agency, one cannot claim that the association's
formalization has ever qualified for inclusion in the
fourth stage of formalization. Furthermore, during the

---

[9]The years 1962 through 1964 are not represented
in this chapter because the minute book convering this
interval is not available. Also, in 1959 the association
began to consider purchasing various buildings which could
serve as a clubhouse. In 1960 the search for such a
structure continued but the members voted not to incur the
expense of breaking their existing five-year lease.
Therefore, the Mexican association did not purchase a
meeting hall until 1965.

period of thirty-four years in which this association has remained at Stage 2, major transformations have occurred in this organization which Tsouderos's model fails to predict. Decline rather than further formalization has prevailed during recent years of the Mexican Aztec Society's history.

Decline

At the end of 1967 the outgoing president thanked the officers and the assembly for their contribution toward making 1967 "the best year for the club since its founding." Subsequently, however, the fortunes of the association declined precipitiously, and by the latter half of 1968 the members were very concerned over the fact that "business is dropping." By 1969 this trend had proceeded so far, that in order to meet expenses, the officers were compelled to request loans from active members after having been denied a commercial loan.

The Mexican Aztec Society's financial problems involved external as well as internal factors. First, the

Mexican American association was competing with other
associations for social members at a time when the general
population of Bethlehem was showing decreasing interest in
club-sponsored entertainment. Second, profits lost through
alleged shortages of cash and inventory, regularly documented in the association's minutes, certainly might have
helped to diminish any competitive advantage which the
association once might have enjoyed.[10] Several informants
blame "hands in the till" for sizeable though unspecified
monetary losses. In this context the informants invariably
mention one particular member, yet neither he nor anyone
else has ever formally been charged with theft. Moreover,
although many Mexican Americans did not wish to press
charges and "give the club a bad name," others criticize
the concealment of such irregularities, feeling that in
this case silence fosters continuing malpractice.

[10]Under Pennsylvania State Law social clubs are
permitted to sell liquor on Sundays while bars and night
clubs are not. This alone provides social clubs with a
considerable source of income.

"Processes" of Formalization[11]

Increasing Differentiation among Member Statuses

Subsequent to 1937 member statuses became further differentiated but only to a limited extent. During the first months of 1937 when the members were creating their association's formal structure, they promptly distinguished active members from members whose dues had been delinquent for ninety days; only active members qualified for financial benefits. Not until 1954 did the general assembly create the less exclusive status of social member for individuals who desired social privileges but either failed to qualify for or did not desire active membership (Chapter IV). However, no additional formal differentiation among member statuses has been instituted by the Mexican Aztec Society. This minimal differentiation among member statuses, too, supports Tsouderos's model, if weakly.

---

[11]I have placed "processes" within quotation marks in order to suggest that the constituent processes of formalization are more accurately considered as indicators that formalization has occurred. Only through decades of participant observation could I have adequately delineated the process of formalization per se.

Growth in Size of the Membership
Body

In the 1950's, attracted by the featured entertainment as well as by the liquor sales--especially the Sunday sale of alcohol which was prohibited to commercial bars and night clubs, numerous applicants for membership soon took advantage of the recently instituted category of social member. Indeed, prominent citizens of the Lehigh Valley as well as members of every conceivable ethnic origin patronized the entertainment offerings now sponsored as a matter of course for a large, heterogeneous social membership. In 1957 alone there were 1,230 applications for social membership, and capacity crowds became commonplace whenever entertainers performed. However, for decades the number of active members remained in the range of 90 to 150. It is the number of social members which grew rapidly-- to a peak of approximately 3,000 in 1966. As predicted by the Tsouderos model, total membership did increase over the associations first three decades of existence.

Attenuation of Communication between Officers and Members

As a corollary of the observation that members of the Mexican Aztec Society have come to interact with one another in progressively more limited contexts, one can observe that the officers are not unlike other members in this regard. While interaction among members has declined, communication between officers and members has also decreased for the same reasons. However, the officers have not become separated from their constituency by an extensive growth and bureaucratization of the association's organizational structure; nor have officers become full time specialists who function as professional executives in addition to their statuses as members. These latter impediments to member-leader communication which Tsouderos predicts have not been operant in the Mexican Aztec Society; however, member-leader communication has indeed decreased.

Changes in Intragroup Relationships

Should Tsouderos' formalization model accurately describe the Mexican Aztec Society, one would observe that

the charter members constituted a primary group. Such a
group is one "in which people come to know one another
intimately as individual personalities" (Horton and Hunt
1968:327). The membership body, as determined by Tsouderos'
model, today constitutes a secondary group, or one in which
"contacts are impersonal, segmented, and utilitarian"
(Ibid.). To some extent, the data support the prediction
that the persons who organized this voluntary association
did then approximate a primary group. Recalling that in
1937 over fifty percent of the charter members resided in
the Labor Camp, one should note that recollections of
former camp residents focus upon the primary group relationships which there obtained: intimate knowledge of all
other camp dwellers; integrative fictive consanguineal, and
affinal kinship bonds among co-residents; customary but
informal modes of mutual cooperation; contexts for satisfying social interactions; and maintenance of social control
by means of gossip and ostracism (vide Chapter II, supra).
Although definitive data are lacking, it appears probable
that a large minority, if not a majority, of the association's

founders did, indeed, constitute a primary group. Convocations have always exhibited the informal social sanctions which derive from the association's sociability function; however the members also created formal mechanisms for social control: eligibility criteria, parliamentary rules or order, codified statements of members' obligations and officers' responsibilities, and provision for ostracism of delinquent members. Furthermore, as a result of participation in the formal voluntary association which had been organized, members began to treat one another more impersonally by virtue of identification of members (individuals) with the membership statuses which they occupied. In 1970, for instance, I have heard members criticize their peers for proposing the impeachment of an unpopular officer: "You elected him, now give him the respect due his office." Moreover, as early as 1950 the president discriminated between his status as member and his associational leadership status of president when he temporarily relinquished the chair in order to freely participate in a highly controversial discussion as a concerned member. In other

words, members do treat person and status separately in
the context of their association.

With the passage of time members have also interacted with one another in increasingly circumscribed
situations, until, at present, many Mexican American
members regularly interact with fellow ethnics only while
in their club, if at all. In this sense, another characteristic of secondary groups applies to the Mexican Aztec
Society: ties among members are highly segmental.
Furthermore, with increasing frequency members participate
in the Mexican Aztec society because of personal instrumental considerations rather than because of the association's expressive functions. Members who state that "I
worked for the club to learn something," or "I stopped
working here because there's no percentage in it" value
the association's utilitarian potential above the pleasures
which could be derived from social relationships with
fellow participants. Indeed, each of these observations
support the hypothesis that the association's membership
body has increasingly come to resemble a secondary group.

Examination of the Mexican Aztec Society's characteristics vis-a-vis primary or secondary groups is further complicated by the fact that a secondary group may be comprised of various primary groups. Within the membership body persons recognize kinship groups and cliques of friends, both primary groups. Therefore, members experience role conflict whenever the obligations of primary relationships, such as kinship, are incompatible with secondary relationships. To illustrate, informants claim that they once attempted to solve a theft problem by forcibly searching a suspected member; however it is said that the association's president forbade this action because of bonds of kinship between himself and the suspect. Similarly, officers who attempt to administer the association in a "businesslike manner" encounter resistance from members who value primary group social relationships above efficiency. Indeed, much of the conflict among association members can be accounted for by the divergent expectations and sanctions employed by primary and secondary groups.

Growing Disaffection of Members
and Decline in Participation

In 1967 the association experienced the first of
several serious financial setbacks which served to high-
light a severe decline in member participation. This
period of decline has by no means been limited to the
area of finance. After having learned to expect
remuneration for nearly all services rendered to this
previously successful commercial venture, few members were
willing to contribute their services to the association in
an era when wages could not be paid. In effect, emphasis
upon commercial expansion severely hampered the possibility
of retrenchment within the association. This need to
retrench, which partially results from conditions not under
the members' control, brought into sharp relief their
differential motivations. With apparent dedication, many
members had formerly helped to operate the club; however
when wages could no longer be paid, their dedication gave
way to considerations of self interest. Others frankly
state that they choose to serve the association "because of

what I can learn"--some men learned bartending in the
club bar and now earn wages bartending elsewhere.[12] "Old
timers" who served the association for a dozen or more
years--gratis--are understandably bitter when they complain
that "no one wants to work any more." For certain members,
therefore, service because of dedication has become
transformed into service motivated by personal instrumental
considerations.

Suggesting a precarious future existence for the
association, several informants claim that at present the
members holding the majority of offices are, in fact, "the
only ones who would take the job."[13] At least during some
periods in the past, it was usual for several persons to
responsibly accept nominations for any given office.
Furthermore, during this "golden era" of participation,
members were sometimes known to decline nominations--not
to shirk their duty but, instead, to permit more able

---

[12]This modification in the orientation of association members appears to reflect a transformation throughout
the colonia in the direction of the American ideals of self-
reliance and hard work being applied to advancing oneself.

[13]Vera Green (1969) has documented a similar
decline in Aruban voluntary associations. Several years
after immigration into Aruba declined the voluntary
associations which functioned for the benefit of immigrants
also became severely weakened.

persons to serve. Moreover, for several years the number
of members who choose active membership, a prerequisite for
all elective status positions, has been declining. In
order to remedy these situations, in 1965 the president
appointed a delegation to seek new active members. One
observes that the recruitment problem is especially grave
given the small size of the colonia and the declining
number of Mexican Americans who identify with their
cultural heritage.

Assuming that meeting attendance provides at least
a gross measure of member participation, one notes that, on
the one hand, an average attendance of approximately thirty
members per meeting occurred only during 1953 to 1955 and
in 1961 while, on the other hand, after 1955 the attendance
figures cluster at near twenty members per meeting, 1961
excepted. In short, attendance at meetings suggests that
most members are willing to leave to others the operation
of their association.[14] Only during the periods when the

------

[14]Instrumental voluntary associations usually
evidence less member participation than do expressive
associations because instrumental matters can generally be
administered by a minority of the members (Barber 1965:
486-487). Therefore, those members who joined the Mexican
association for instrumental reasons could not be expected
to participate as actively as the members who derive more
satisfaction for its expressive functions.

Mexican Aztec Society was about to experience some type of expansion did numerous members enthusiastically participate in association affairs. Soon after the association moved into permanent quarters in 1952, attendance rose and maintained a high level through 1953, when the association became incorporated and licensed to sell liquor. However, this high rate of attendance was sustained for only two additional years. Not until 1961 when members began to search for a structure which could be purchased for a clubhouse did interest in the association again quicken. Although at least some second-generation Mexican Americans may have become active participants in association affairs. Because of personal instrumental motivations, for example, in order to gain experience in business matters or to acquire occupational skills, perhaps the more general explanation of these peaks in association activity lies in the enhancement of Mexican American ethnic pride which has accrued from each of the Mexican Aztec Society major accomplishments. Indeed, informants proudly inform the researcher that the Mexican Aztec Society is the only

Mexican American voluntary association in the eastern
United States which owns its own clubhouse.

Members have, in fact, attained a level of
participation in their association which approximates that
of most associations located in the United States; however
association members have neither sustained intense nor even
constant levels of participant in their organization.
After approximately 1965 decline in members' willingness to
contribute to the maintenance of the Mexican Aztec Society
has alarmed those members who most value "the club."

Summary

Utilization of the Tsouderos formalization model
as an heuristic framework partially illuminates organizational and other transformations which transpired within
Bethlehem's Mexican American voluntary associations during
the past forty years. As predicted by Tsouderos, an initial
stage of informal association (Stage 1) preceded the
formation of the Mexican Aztec Society in 1937 (Stage 2)
which included the codification of election procedure and
the creation of formal leadership statuses. However,

despite ample evidence for further formalization this association has never fully qualified for the model's Stage 3: never did the members create a professional leadership status, although the steward (more appropriately considered as a bartender than as an association executive) was paid a salary for several years. Nor did the Mexican Aztec Society advance to Stage 4 or Stage 5 after omitting Stage 3: the Mexican association has not segmented into various associations which recognize a centralized control. Therefore, it has not been necessary to tighten the control of a central executive over nonexistent constituent organizations. Much as attempts at revitalization may traverse but a subset of the revitalization process (Wallace 1970:188-199), the case of the Mexican Aztec Society establishes the fact that formalization of voluntary associations may cease long before they become highly formal and bureaucratized via successive transformations from Stage 1 to Stages 2, 3, 4, and then 5.

According to Tsouderos one can resolve the formalization process into several interdependent components. The

data provide some indication that the Mexican Aztec Society
has manifested each component: (1) An increased differentiation among membership statuses occurred after nearly
twenty years of associational activity when the general
assembly instituted social membership in addition to the
category of active membership; (2) The membership body
increased in size from less than one hundred to approximately 3000; (3) to some extent, communication between
officers and members has become attenuated; (4) The
membership body has decreasingly resembled a primary group;
however, although members now resemble a secondary group,
primary groups also exist within the membership body;
(5) Members have decreasingly evidenced a disaffection
with the association and, accordingly, their participation
has also declined.

The Mexican Aztec Society has become formalized to
much less an extent than that predicted by the Tsouderos
model; however the predictions which apply to the initial
stages have been supported by the data. Moreover, future
events could conceivably propel this Mexican American

voluntary association into increased formalization. For
these reasons this test supports a subset of the model
while neither proving nor disproving the remainder.
Further extensive research would be necessary to test the
model's cross cultural validity.

However, despite consistency between the Tsouderos
model and the present data, sole dependence upon this model
as an heuristic framework for the diachronic description of
Mexican American voluntarism causes one to ignore important
aspects of the empirical case. Utilization of this framework focuses one's attention upon gross descriptive
regularities to the neglect of the numerous functions
served by the Mexican Aztec Society--the subject which I
shall treat in Chapter IV.

CHAPTER IV

ASSOCIATIONAL FUNCTIONS OF THE MEXICAN

AZTEC SOCIETY: 1937-1970

Hypothesized Associational
Functions

Perusal of numerous descriptions of voluntary
associations which are located throughout the world leads
to the conclusion that several associational functions are
so consistently identified that each of these functions
warrants examination for applicability to the case of
Bethlehem's Mexican Aztec Society (vide Chapter I).
(1) Voluntary associations organized by rural-urban or
international migrants initially provide members with
illness or bereavement benefits. Such has been the case
throughout the Azteca's entire history.

(2) Urban associations are said to "cushion" the
changes imposed upon migrants by providing them with a
"cultural bridge" (vide Chapter I). Only for a minority of
members has their voluntary association served this function.

By 1937 when Mexicans organized the association most members of their _colonia_ had already resided in Bethlehem for a decade or more. Therefore, rather than the Mexican Aztec Society, the Mexican associations which temporally preceded the present organization existed during the era when most first generation Mexican immigrants needed a cultural bridge. However, during the 1950's and the 1960's more recent immigrants from Mexico to Bethlehem did utilize the association's potention function as cultural bridge. Indeed, despite the small numbers of such arrivals, these "new Mexicans" constitute a large minority of the members who most actively participate in association activities. For these individuals the cultural continuity provided by the Mexican association continues to be desirable.

(3) Voluntary associations are also said to socialize members into unaccustomed modes of behavior which have recently become appropriate for them (_vide_ Chapter I). To some extent, participation in the Mexican Aztec Society has performed a socialization function. The members

acquired the rudiments of parliamentary procedure and the
elective leaders learned yet more; they learned to interact
with leaders of other associations, politicians, lawyers,
and various public officials in addition to acquiring
expertise in their official duties. For example, in perusal
of the minutes of meetings, I have noted that over a period
of several years some secretaries appreciably improved both
their spelling and their style of writing. Also, because
of the experience gained from discharging the responsibilities of elective offices within the Mexican Aztec
Society, several members have later utilized their leadership skills within yet other organizations. However, only
rarely do unacculturated Mexican immigrants--persons who
may acutely need a cultural bridge--apply for membership.
Therefore, no major need has ever compeled the association
to emphasize members' socialization into American modes of
behavior.

(4) Voluntary associations flexibly permit members
to either intensify or extend their social networks (vide
Chapter I). Initially, through their participation

association members only intensified existing links in
their personal social networks. Until the middle 1950's,
members almost invariably already knew all other participants and therefore utilized this associational
opportunity to "cement" certain bonds. However, during the
1950's and the 1960's the association's commercial interests
necessitated officers' contacts with journalists, businessmen, attorneys, politicians, and others. As a consequence
of their official duties Mexican Aztec Society leaders
extended their social networks. Furthermore, because of
the explosive growth in the number of social members during
the late 1950's, in the context of association activities
many Mexican Americans came into contact with large numbers
of persons of diverse origins, thus also widening their
social networks.

(5) Voluntary associations may provide members
with opportunities for social or economic mobility (vide
Chapter I). Several members who learned bartending as
volunteer workers for the association have since supplemented their income as steel workers by working part time

as professional bartenders in local bars and nightclubs.
One Mexican American who has obtained a state level labor
union office reports that he was able to do so because of
the leadership experience which he gained while serving the
Azteca. Area politicians sometimes approach one particular
Mexican American in order to encourage him to run for
political office; because this individual is president of
the Bethlehem Clubmen's Association and because he holds
an office in the Mexican Aztec Society, non-Mexican
Americans present him with these opportunities for social
and economic mobility.

     (6) Voluntary associations also serve as sources
of unity which to some extent compensate for internal
conflicts (vide Chapter I). Indeed, the Mexican Americans
no longer have any organized source of unity except the
Mexican Aztec Society. At least a decade ago Mexican
Americans ceased to attend Holy Infancy Roman Catholic
Church which had once provided a "Mexican church" in its
basement.

In August of 1963, the sport of baseball provided Bethlehem's Mexican Americans with an opportunity to proudly manifest their cultural heritage as well as some semblance of unity. In the Little League Senior Division World Series held in Bethlehem during that period a team from Monterrey, Mexico became world champions while at the same time endearing themselves to the local populace. In attempting to make the Little Leaguers feel at home, old and young Mexican Americans received them with "banner, sombreros and Mexican music" (Bethlehem Globe-Time k) followed later by a celebration at the association's club-house complete with national dishes and music.

The opportunities for Bethlehem residents to lavish kindness upon the ill-equipped Monterrey team served to augment the warmth of local feelings for these youths. For example, while the team was touring the Bethlehem Steel Corporation plant, the company's mechanics were overhauling the engine of their typically Mexican bus, repairing the fuel tank and the fuel pump, straightening the frame, and mounting six new tires (Morning Call). Previously according

to the Mexican Little League's interpreter "the bus performed real well going downhill but there are too many
places in this country that also require a bus to go
uphill" (Ibid.). Then, when it was learned that the boys
from Monterrey owned only three bats and a few baseballs,
the Mexican Aztec Society purchased for them the set of
equipment with which they became the World Champions.[1]
These and innumerable other smaller kindnesses were heaped
upon the Monterrey team by Bethlehem's residents, Anglos
and Latins alike. Indeed, the members' enthusiastic
welcome of the boys from Monterrey, Mexico, with _fiestas_
at the clubrooms and a cheering section at the ballpark,
constitutes a major public manifestation of the unity of
Bethlehem's Mexican Americans. Aztecans' participation in
this local event was not only well-publicized but also
approved by other Bethlehemites.

To some extent each of the six functions often
attributed to voluntary associations do also apply to the
Mexican Aztec Society; however, except for the mutual
assistance function, each of the six pertain only to

[1]"Monterey, Mexico World Champions of Little League
Senior Division Baseball" [Clipping, no information]
(Bethlehem Globe-Times 1).

relatively small numbers of members or to the association

as a whole at a very limited time period. Therefore,

further examination of the association's functions is called

for in order to better comprehend the forces which motivated

the members to maintain their association for forty-four

years. I shall begin by testing several functions which

have been postulated as attributes of Mexican American

voluntary associations.[2]

Functions Particular to Mexican American Voluntary Associations

Informational and Communication Networks

Interaction among members while participating in

association activities facilitates the flow of information

among Mexican Americans as well as generally providing

opportunities for human communication. Regular meetings of

the general assembly and of the Ladies Auxiliary in addition

to the events which are scheduled for the purpose of

entertainment permit one a context for exchange of information

---

[2]Four out of the five functions have been postulated by a Mexican American social scientist. The remaining function was originally suggested by Treudley (1966) as an attribute of the Greek American voluntary associations of Boston.

about employment, "gossip" and other matters of mutual
interest. Only rarely do the participants depart
immediately upon the termination of a meeting; instead they
remain to drink and converse with one another. For the
occasional recent immigrant from Mexico, information about
potential jobs, as well as assistance from members, can be
obtained as a result of attendance at gatherings held in
the clubhouse. Furthermore, the Mexican Aztec Society
provides for some communication between Mexican Americans
and politicians or local organizations. For example, free
chest x-rays have been made available to Mexican Americans
via the association. Similarly, members become aware of
local politicians' stands upon various issues when the
politicians speak at official association affairs.

Interaction Among Mexican Americans

Participation in the Mexican Aztec Society does
cause members to interact who would not otherwise come into
contact with one another. Just as in Boston, where the
Greek Americans no longer share a common residential

location, during the past twenty years, Mexican Americans
of Bethlehem have dispersed throughout the city. Therefore, barring kinsmen and co-workers, Mexican Americans
rarely encounter groups of fellow ethnics except when they
attend activities of the Mexican Aztec Society. Only
occasionally do funerals or weddings also cause reunions
among dozens of Mexican Americans. Indeed, in a newspaper
interview held in 1966, the president of the Mexican Aztec
Society explicitly stated that his voluntary association
establishes "a central meeting-place for persons of
Mexican origin" (Bethlehem Globe-Times m). In summary,
the Mexican association latently functions to provide some
small measure of cohesion within a colonia mexicana which
is no longer approximately contiguous geographically.

Source of Varied Organizational Opportunities

Because more than one formally organized Mexican
American voluntary association has yet to exist there
simultaneously, Bethlehem's Mexican-Americans have never
been provided with a variety of opportunities for voluntarism.

In contrast, the numerous Mexican American voluntary associations found in San Antonio, Texas (Lane 1968) or Tucson, Arizona (Officer 1964) do provide for this function. Furthermore, despite some unsuccessful attempts at creating several specialized functions under the aegis of the Mexican Aztec Society (vide Chapter III), this voluntary association has continued to offer its members only a few generalized functions rather than encompassing several alternatives. In both regards, the Mexican Aztec Society fails to provide a variety of organizational opportunities; however unlike some cities of the Southwest, Mexican Americans in Bethlehem have wide opportunities to join local Anglo associations.

Preservation of Mexican American Culture

Although the Mexican Aztec Society does indeed preserve aspects of Mexican American culture, little evidence suggests that members have overtly directed the association's activities toward this goal. During World War II, the general assembly voted to establish a Mexican

library and to instruct members' children in Mexican
history and the Spanish language; however, these plans were
never operationalized. The principal aspects of Mexican
American culture which members do consciously strive to
maintain are the annual observances of Mexican patriotic
holidays.

Framework for Cultural Pluralism

The Mexican Aztec Society does indeed provide
members with a context in which they can appropriately
manifest cultural pluralism. On the one hand, second
generation Mexican American members invariably can behave
in ways judged by Anglos as proper for "Americans." On
the other hand, both first and second generation Mexican
Americans also manifest behaviors which reflect some
influence of Mexican culture. Because members of Bethlehem's
Mexican colony organized a Mexican Aztec Society, this
voluntary association, almost by definition, constitutes a
pluralistic framework. As Frederik Barth states (1969:
14-15), "an ethnic group persists only as long as

individuals continue to _identify_ themselves as members of
that ethnic group." Furthermore, the participation of
Mexican Americans in the Azteca association does indeed
constitute their personal identification as both "Mexican"
and "American."

Membership in this association implies identification as Mexican, but members must be citizens of the United
States in order to qualify for formal leadership statuses
and, moreover, members occasionally remind me that "we're
also American." In other words, an extension of Barth's
ideas about the maintenance of ethnic boundaries leads to
the conclusion that the Mexican Aztec Society provides a
pluralistic framework because of identifications with both
Mexican _and_ American cultures.

The Mexican voluntary association also constitutes
a pluralistic framework on account of its admixture of
cultural elements. Despite the initial prevalent use of
Spanish both for discussions and also for the keeping of
records, in recent years both Spanish and English have
characterized members' discussions. Although the

half-dozen "old timers" who attend the Azteca meetings are
able to speak English, in contrast with the second generation Mexican Americans who usually speak English, these
"old timers" usually address the assembly in Spanish.
Cases in which younger Mexican Americans converse in
Spanish include discussions directed to the respected and
elderly Sr. Anastasio Tejeda. Indeed, I have observed a
second generation Mexican American launch into a speech in
Spanish, stop to ask in English "how do you say _____,"
receive an answer, and then continue on in Spanish despite
the fact that Sr. Tejeda actually knows this word in
English. The use of Spanish in this situation follows
from habit in the customs of respect for elders. At other
times the language shifts repeatedly after a short exchange
in the same language in which the topic of discussion was
initiated.

As for the cultural content of the association's
entertainment offerings, a previously Mexican repertoire of
music and cinema gave way in the 1950's to a mixture of
the "Mexican" and the "American." Whenever possible, the

association hired _mariachi_ bands from New York City.
However, performances of local non-Mexican orchestras
became more frequent. During recent years, the members
have reserved Saturday evening for _Latin_ music while
engaging "rock bands" Friday and Sunday (_vide_ Chapter V).

The Mexican American voluntary associations in
Bethlehem (one) clearly do not offer a source of varied
organizational opportunities. However, this association
does facilitate communication among members, encourage
interaction among Mexican Americans, seek to preserve
Mexican American culture, and provide a framework for
cultural pluralism. Nevertheless, this list does not
encompass the functions which the field data suggest most
strongly.

Functions of the Mexican Aztec Society

Manifest Functions

The association's founders chose to promulgate both
instrumental and expressive functions of their voluntary
association:

> The objects [sic] for which this society
> strives are the following: to be of mutual
> help and to foment amongst our members the
> spirit of solidarity and fellowship; to
> render assistance to sick members and to
> their families in case of death (By-laws).

In establishing an instrumental association which provided

for health and bereavement benefits, the Mexicans followed

a course which rural-urban migrants have adopted within

widespread locations throughout the world (Chapter I).

But, members also desired to overcome the division within

the colonia mexicana which resulted from their diverse

origins in Mexico; they envisaged the Mexican Aztec Society

as an association which could foster increased social

solidarity of Mexicans while also providing for sociability.

Indeed, they also selected Unión y Fraternidad (Unity and

Fraternity) as their association's motto. Furthermore,

other statements of purpose recorded in the association's

minutes of meetings establish that members also planned to

"foster good relations with the Spanish and Portuguese

colonies" of Bethlehem by means of the association's

activities. Without doubt, the founders intended to

augment social solidarity by bringing members into periodic

contact with one another and by organizing festivities

for all local speakers of Spanish and Portuguese.

In years subsequent to the Mexican Aztec Society

founding, the voluntary association's leaders have made

slightly different statements about their organization's

functions. To illustrate, an application for incorporation

as a nonprofit organization which was filed in 1942,

reiterated the mutual assistance and social solidarity

functions which had originally been promulgated by the

association's charter members; however, they also appended

a phrase not consistent with "traditional" Mexican culture:

"to use its [the association's] influence to increase the

love for work." One might infer that the members inserted

that phrase upon advice of legal council in order to please

the presiding judge with evidence for the Protestant work

ethic. The emphasis upon production which characterized

the era of World War II could also have inspired inclusion

of this clause. However, from the association's first year

of existence the members limited payment of health benefits

to cases in which a member is unable to <u>work</u>. In one of
the possible interpretations of this ruling, members are
officially encouraged to value work. Furthermore, by 1970,
many Mexican Americans of Bethlehem have, indeed, adopted a
work ethic. These observations lead to the inference that
the members may well have seriously intended to foster a
"love for work" by means of their voluntary association.
Nevertheless, only because of its expressive functions
could the Mexican Aztec Society's several instrumental
functions be successfully achieved.

Avoidance of Social Action

Often one observes that voluntary association are
organized for the instrumental purpose of instituting
social change programs which further the member's special
interests (Hammond 1972:15-18). However, the Mexican
Aztec Society is noteworthy for having studiously avoided
supporting any of the political factions which had vied
for power in Mexico. Furthermore, within the context of
the Mexican Aztec Society, the members were expressly

forbidden by the association's constitution to engage in any discussions which dealt with matters of politics or religion.[3] Apparently, the Mexicans who founded the association recognized that the topics of politics and religion, which had caused such strife in Mexico, could only cause dissention among themselves. It is also clear that topics of politics and religion were actively discussed outside the Azteca.

During 1937, members of the Mexican Aztec Society repeatedly reaffirmed their desire to dissociate their organization from all political contexts. In their interpretation, this rule precluded the association's cooperation with the Frente Popular Anti-Facista (Popular Anti-Facist Front) of Bethlehem's Spanish colonia. However, the temptation to support political activities was strong; some Spaniards were dues-paying members of the Mexican Aztec Society, while many others often attended social activities held by the Mexican association. Nevertheless,

---

[3]Although discussions of religion, in addition to politics, are forbidden in all Mexican association contexts, in 1939 the assembly granted a member the gratis use of the rented room for a celebration of the feast day of Mexico's patron saint--the Virgin of Guadalupe. Moreover, from time to time the association provided other minor support for religious functions.

the Mexicans steadfastly maintained their ideals. In
fact, they even felt compelled to decline the offer of
free use of a hall for a dance which they wished to hold
because the invitation had been extended by the <u>Frente</u>
<u>Popular</u>. Apparently activities of this anti-facist
organization declined after Franco's victory in Spain, so
that the political proscriptions of the Mexican Aztec
Society's by-laws ceased to strain relations between
Mexicans and local Spaniards. Indeed, only in a single
known instance has the Mexican Aztec Society attempted to
influence the actions of politicians while discharging
the function of Mexican American defense association. In
1954, following the attack which a group of Puerto Rican
radicals made upon the United States House of Representatives, a Congressman representing the Lehigh Valley, is
said to have used the term "scummy" when comparing Mexicans
(or Mexican Americans?) to the Spanish speaking attackers.
In defense of their compatriots, the Mexican Aztec Society
responded with indignation by calling upon this politician
to issue a public apology. To the members' dismay, the

gentleman sidestepped the entire issue in his reply;
however, association members did not pursue their demand
for remedial action.

A decade ago the Mexican Aztec Society's general
assembly declined to serve in a mediative capacity between
the Immigration Department and Mexicans seeking to reside
in Bethlehem. As Paul Taylor observed in 1930 (1931b)
numerous Mexican residents of Bethlehem had been able to
settle in Pennsylvania because of the assistance provided
by their kinsmen already in residence there. However, with
the advent of the Great Depression, Mexican immigration to
Bethlehem ceased, never to be resumed with the same magnitude. In 1961, when a person employed by the Immigration
Department promised to "help bring members of our families
to this country," the general assembly filed the information
for future reference rather than utilizing the proferred
assistance.

In 1954, the Mexican Aztec Society successfully
mobilized a portion of Bethlehem's population in support of
a Mexican family which was facing deportation by the

Immigration and Naturalization Bureau. The wife involved
in this case had been born in Bethlehem but returned as a
child to Mexico and then eventually returned again to
Bethlehem with her Mexican husband and children. A
problem arose because the husband had lived in Bethlehem
for four years on a six month visitor's visa: having been
apprehended by the authorities, he was liable to deportation. At the behest of the association many residents of
Bethlehem, including local and state political figures,
petitioned that this man be permitted to become an American
citizen. However, only rarely did this Mexican voluntary
association attempt to effect the actions of non-members
through application of its influence and power.

Nevertheless, at least once the members have voted
to donate an evening's income to César Chávez's strike
fund, thus supporting the social action of the National
Farmworkers Union. The members readily identify with this
struggle to obtain "fair" working conditions, but they
generally find the brown power movement distasteful. One
hears "they [militant Mexican Americans] want something for

nothing just like the Negroes. I worked for what I've got."
Belief in self-reliance prevents most members from participating in any social action voluntary associations which
made demands on the basis of individuals' ethnicity rather
than their achievements. Indeed, in Bethlehem, Mexican
American belief in self-reliance applies especially to the
realm of public assistance.

Both Mexican American informants and a local social
worker agree that local Mexican Americans do not request
public assistance funds except in extreme situations where
there is no other alternative. Hence, except during the
Great Depression, very few Mexican Americans have received
public assistance. One informant supported this assertion
by describing an analogous situation in San Antonio, Texas:

> During the depression an employment office was
> located in the same block as the food distribu-
> tion center. The Mexicans invariably went first
> to the employment office waiting there until
> several hours later, when the last job had been
> assigned. Only then would the Mexicans walk
> down the street to join the line for the food
> dole.

In short, the informant wished to imply that Mexican
Americans accept public assistance with a reluctance at

least the equal of that observed in San Antonio.

Communication with Mexicans Who
Reside Elsewhere in the
United States

In addition to serving a communication function for members, the Mexican Aztec Society has also facilitated communication among Mexican colonies. The secretary has corresponded with Mexican associations which are located as distantly as Saginaw, Michigan, and, moreover, received a newsletter from this organization. Also, without the slightest indication that any member feared the possibility of dishonesty, association officers sold raffle tickets for a trip to Mexico which a Mexican association in Toledo, Ohio, had sponsored (a resident of Toledo won the prize). However, contacts with Mexican colonias of Philadelphia, New York, and nearby Palmerton predominated. Especially during the 1940's the Mexican Aztec Society maintained close contacts with the Mexican voluntary association in Palmerton. Periodically one organization extended invitations to social events to members of the other colonia.

For example, in 1941, the Sociedad Mutualista Latino
Americana (Latin American Mutual Society) of Palmerton
invited the Aztecans to a dance in order to celebrate the
Palmerton association's third anniversary. Despite the
small size of the colonia in Palmerton, informants emphasize
that in order to enhance the festivities, the association
had engaged a Mexican orchestra from Philadelphia. Another
Mexican voluntary association, Unión Cultural Mexicana, of
New York City also maintained enduring ties with the
Mexican Aztec Society. Indeed, photographs preserved
within the association's files establish that the Unión
Cultural Mexicana sponsored a large Mariachi band (eleven
persons) comprised of members who upon several occasions
attired themselves in traditional Mexican costumes while
performing for the Mexican Aztec Society. Furthermore, for
decades, the Mexican Aztec Society has provided hospitality
to a busload of Unión Cultural Mexicana members who traveled
to Bethlehem for a picnic at Saucon Park followed by a
visit to the Mexican association for drink, dance, and
conversation with compatriots.

As the Mexican Consul's chief contact with
Bethlehem's Mexican Americans, the Sociedad Mexicana Azteca
periodically received inquiries from the consul concerning
various Mexicans. Indeed, to facilitate communication with
Mexican American residents of Bethlehem in 1943, the consul
requested and was granted an "honorary representative"
from the colonia. As illustration of the consul's queries,
in 1950, the association was asked for information concerning the whereabouts of a Mexican who had run away from
home in 1934, at the age of twenty-three; a mother wished
to find her missing son. In another case, a Mexican not
belonging to the association, died in Bethlehem after
having been struck by a train. At the Mexicans Consul's
request, the officers of the Sociedad Azteca Mexicana
investigated the circumstances of this man's death, learning that any property that he had owned had been willed to
local friends of the deceased--to one Portuguese and to
one Mexican. One notes with interest that the officers
offered the opinion that the deceased's relatives (if any)
in his birthplace of Uruapan, Michoacán should receive his

property. Needless to say, the Mexican Consul agreed that
a local Portuguese has much less right to any such property
or savings than does a Mexican three thousand miles away.

Health Benefits or Social Control?

Significantly, the Mexican association operates as
an agency of colonia social control. For example, consensual
unions, "excesses," and other immoralities were publically
condemned by members of the association during their formal
meetings. Similarly, exemplary behavior, such as devoted
service of certain officers, was praised and sometimes
rewarded with monetary tribute. At times it is difficult
to determine whether the association serves more as an
agency for social control or as an association dedicated to
the payment of sickness and death benefits. From the
voluntary association's inception, members defined their
duties in universalistic terms which could easily be
applied to efforts at social control. As stated in the
by-laws, "Members shall attend all assemblies whether
ordinary [regular] or extra ordinary [special] . . . attend

the funeral of deceased [members] of this society . . .
attend all meetings in full control of their mental
faculties." Members discovered that they could not enforce
the norm of required attendance; however the requirement
that members attend meeting "in full control of their
mental faculties" lent itself to some social control of the
use of intoxicants by members. Also, on threat of expulsion
any officer contemplating resignation from his post was
required to show due cause for his purported inability to
discharge his official responsibilities. As recently as
1965, the association's general assembly ruled that all
fights were to be made public at each regular meeting thus
facilitating informal sanctions against the participants.

Once the Mexican American voluntary association
could legally sell liquor, the number of members expelled
for "improper conduct" became noteworthy. Also, it became
customary for transgressing members to convey their
apologies to the assembly while, at the same time, begging
forgiveness for their disruptive behavior. For example, as
recorded by the secretary, a member who "ran after the

doorman with a knife realized his mistake and asked the society to decide his case." Informants relate that several of the expulsions during the 1950's concerned fights between Puerto Ricans and Mexican Americans. In any case, the association's officers felt compelled to hire off-duty policemen to act as "bouncers" on weekend nights. Moreover, in 1957, an association official proposed that "all doormen should get paid for any shirts torn when there are fights in the club"; proposal endorsed.

Perhaps 1938 is outstanding because of the several instances of moralizing recorded in the association's minutes for that year. To cite one example, in a discussion of eligibility for sick benefits it was decided that members should not receive benefits for an illness "due to excess or a shameful reason." However, preoccupation with the morals of members is not confined to the '30's, for in later years the legality of a marital union was sometimes questioned. For example, in 1966, a member suggested that two Mexicans in particular be granted active membership only if the couple presented a valid marriage certificate.

Obviously, members of the society feared that they would be compelled to pay benefits for disabilities incurred through "sexual excesses," alcoholism, or other "immoral" behavior. Although the association's minutes never define what is meant by "immoral behavior"; one can observe that much moral indignation did result, for example, from instances of conjugal pairs living in consensual union.

However, sanctions against moral deviance do not always prevent the assembly from making decisions which conflict with the association's by-laws. Periodically the members vote to award benefits to persons whose eligibility is denied by the association's constitution or by the assembly's earlier ruling. The members apply informal negative sanctions of a verbal nature more often than they institute formal negative sanctions of an economic nature. In 1949, the members proved their inability to strictly enforce the association's regulations concerning benefits. A woman had joined the society after having known for two years that she had an incurable disease. It was not until after this member died that the association's assembly

learned of this woman's medical history, and of her
fraudulent statement of "good health." A long argument
ensued concerning whether or not death benefits due to her
survivors should be paid in the face of such flagrant
dishonesty. Eventually, after a tied vote, the officers
broke the tie by voting to disburse the benefits to her
surviving spouse. However, this did not end the controversy; in the following meeting a prominent member
demanded without success that the woman's "spouse" be
expelled for never having formally married her! Thus, it
seems that for good reason one informant recalls this
incident as having been the most sensitive and divisive
development experienced by the Mexican Aztec Society during
its first dozen years.

Although details of the situation are quite different, another strong controversy developed among members,
this time following the death of an officer's wife. In
this case, the particular officer concerned had served the
association for many years. After his wife, who had never
been a member, died following the accumulation of numerous

medical expenses, thirty members (a previously unheard of number) petitioned for a special meeting at which this case might be considered. After lengthy and heated discussion--in which the president temporarily relinquished his chair in order to speak from the floor--the assembly finally voted to "donate" $100.00 to the officer in light of his service to the association and the fact that he could have directed his wife to become a member, since no one knew of her illness.

These two cases present an ironic contrast. In the former case, because fraud was suspected, the payment of the death benefits to the surviving spouse was hotly debated. In the latter case, however, a delegation of members wished to award a death benefit, despite the fact that the deceased had never been a dues-paying member! Although in each case the final outcome was identical-- benefits were paid--in the former case the dishonesty of the deceased member was of paramount importance, while in the latter case, the honesty of the officer and his deceased wife was a crucial point. These incidents, then

illustrate the fact that decision-making within the
association often evidences moralizing intermixed with
personalism.

Incipient Specialized Functions

Although the Mexican Aztec Society has never
organized branch associations, either in this or other
colonias mexicanas, the members have repeatedly attempted
to differentiate their association, which is characterized
by rather general functions, into several less inclusive
organizations which would serve special interests but,
nevertheless, would also remain under the aegis of the
association. In 1948, the association's general assembly
created the Youth Club of the Mexican Aztec Society for the
purpose of preparing second generation Mexican Americans
to eventually become adult members of their association.
To this end, the "youths" were instructed to hold their
monthly meetings following the association's regular
meetings in order to provide them with an opportunity to
observe the workings of the adults' voluntary association.

However, the "youths" showed little interest and therefore
did not form an enduring "Youth Club." After the association acquired permanently rented quarters (rather than
hiring a hall for each meeting), in 1952 a number of
"youngsters" sought membership but insisted upon their
own funds and board of directors. In this case, the
general assembly vetoed this request on the grounds that
fragmentation of their organization into two autonomous
associations "would foster division within the community
and will be a violation of our motto: Union and Fraternity."
Therefore, second generation Mexican Americans were faced
with the prospects of either declining to affiliate with
the Mexican Aztec Society or joining an association which
their parental generation controlled. By not reorganizing
the association to accommodate the special interests which
were developing in the colonia based upon generational
barriers, the general assembly undermined its future success
in the recruitment of members. At a time when Mexican
Americans were beginning to choose residences in neighborhoods inhabited by few if any fellow ethnics, the Mexican

Aztec Society could have strengthened the "Youth Club" as a means of establishing friendships among second generation Mexican Americans which, in turn, might eventually have led to recruitment into the association as adult members. In 1970, few Mexican American adolescents count more than one or two Mexican Americans among their friends; therefore, adolescents are not today encouraged by their peer groups to become members and association recruitment suffers as a consequence.

In 1947, a civic-minded officer of the Mexican Aztec Society attempted to interest the general assembly in organizing a credit cooperative for the benefit of members. However, despite his success in founding credit cooperatives within two locals of the United Steelworkers of America, members ignored his arguments when they declined to extend their association's mutual benefit function to the realm of finance. However, members have generously responded to suggestions which involve expansion of the association's expressive functions. During most years following 1955 the Mexican Aztec Society has sponsored

at least one athletic team for members or their children.
Furthermore, the association provided the capital necessary
to construct locker and shower facilities for the athletes.
Although teams have been active during additional years,
the association's minutes of meetings establish the
existence of the following teams: soccer (1956-1959),
basketball (1957), baseball (1968), little league baseball
(1966-1969), and darts (1967-1969).

Despite past allegations that an autonomous sub-
association would destroy the association's unity, in
1954 the female members organized a Ladies Auxiliary.
These women, who serve in the clubhouse as waitresses and
cooks, collectively contribute their proceeds to the
association's funds; this source of funds became of the
utmost importance during the late 1960's when finances were
in dire straits. In addition to the auxiliary's instrumental functions in support of the association, this female
association also provides for expressive functions; following their monthly meetings, the women engage in card
playing--a sociability function.

Although Mexican American children are denied membership in the Mexican Aztec Society, several members have, nevertheless maintained a voluntary association for Mexican American children. In 1967, concerned that few Mexican American children were learning Mexican culture, Ann Montoya organized a traditionally costumed folk dance group for Mexican American adolescents. Through this group, named El Grupo Mexicano, Ann gave the children "an opportunity to feel Mexican by dancing and listening to Mexican music." Although Ann strove for authenticity in the dance and in the costumes, her approach conflicted with the ideas of the group's members; the girls wanted mini-skirts rather than long skirts and the boys wanted fitted trousers rather than baggy Mexican trousers (calzones). Yet although many of the dancers' parents had strongly encouraged their children to join El Grupo Mexicano, the parents did not insist that their children accept the authentic regional costumes. Finally, during a serious illness Ann asked another Mexican American woman to manage the group. El Grupo Mexicano has continued to perform for

four years, appearing on at least one local television
broadcast. El Grupo has also made more than two dozen
appearances before the Eastern Star (at all six chapters in
the Lehigh Valley), four church banquets, four P.T.A.
organizations, the Mexican Aztec Society, and other local
voluntary associations. At present, the nine members
range in age from fifteen to twenty years. The Mexican
Aztec Society donated funds to El Grupo when this youth
association was being organized; however, only unofficial
ties connect El Grupo with the association: the members
practice and perform on the Mexican Aztec Society's
premises and many of the children's parents "belong to the
club." Therefore, despite the Azteca's continuing informal
support of El Grupo, it is several Mexican Americans
individuals rather than the Mexican Aztec Society which
organized and now maintains this association of adolescents.

Maurice Freedman's observation, that the number of
specialized voluntary associations in a population is
proportional to the scale and complexity of the population
(1967:47-48), requires some qualification for the case of

Bethlehem. Despite growth in their numbers since the
Great Depression, the Mexican Americans have never instituted more than one formally organized voluntary association. Nevertheless, Freedman's principle holds for
Bethlehem's ethnic groups as a whole; there are several
dozen ethnic voluntary associations of diverse specialized
functions. Apparently the small number of Mexican
Americans (700) and the yet much smaller number of Mexican
Americans who identify with Mexico partially explain why
numerous associations have not been formed. Unlike the
Mexican Americans, most other groups of immigrants residing
in Bethlehem number in thousands of persons. As another
partial explanation, provided that they are eligible as
members, Mexican Americans need not form their own specialized associations if organization serving specialized
functions already exist in Bethlehem. As illustration,
Mexican Americans have not created a parent-teacher association because many already exist which accept them as members.
In summary, both the limited size of the colonia and the
associational opportunities to be found outside of their

colonia have obviated the need for additional formally organized Mexican American voluntary associations whether independent of or a part of the Mexican Aztec Society.

Symbolic Function

Throughout the Mexican Aztec Society's entire history, one can attribute to this association a manifest symbolic function associated with the members' Mexican origins. Members express this organization's symbolic function by means of Mexican patriotism and identification with Mexican culture. Always the celebration of the two most cherished Mexican patriotic holidays, May 5 and September 16, has eclipsed all other social events which the association has organized during each annual cycle.[4] For several years subsequent to 1937, the association held dances in order to commemorate these occasions, also hosting the Spanish and Portuguese colonias. For several years following 1945, they provided the additional and symbolic attraction of Mexican films on these occasions. Until the mid 1950's, the association directed its patriotic

[4] On May 5 Mexicans celebrate the Mexican victory at Puebla over Maximillian's armies in 1862. On September 16, 1821 Mexico declared her independence of Spain.

festivities toward the colonia mexicana and other persons
of hispanic tradition; however in subsequent years, the
celebrations became large commercial affairs for which the
members sometimes engaged large mariachi bands from New
York City. During this recent period of time, the Mexican
Americans hosted several hundred social members of diverse
ethnicity. Despite the preservation of these customs,
however, second generation Mexican American officers have
not internalized a full comprehension of their symbolic
import.

Each year the association sponsored "Mexican Day"
at an amusement park and the Spanish-speaking congregation
of Holy Infancy organized a second similar outing. From
informants' descriptions, both of these annual events seem
to have been rather similar. For each the price of
admission also included food and beer; it is said that
women were charged less than were men because they did not
drink beer or drank it with moderation. Always the pro-
moter's expenses included the cost of hiring a policeman to
maintain order for the day "so that there would be no

complaints," as one informant explained. During the more
elaborate picnics, the Mexican Americans could also view
Mexican films and Mexican performers from New York City.
Both annual outings were last held during the 1950's;
however as patriotic occasions which attracted hundreds of
persons the impacts upon colonia social solidarity were
considerable.

In 1952, the ceremonial bestowal of a charter of
incorporation by the Commonwealth of Pennsylvania illustrates the opportunities provided to Mexican Aztec Society
members for symbolic expression of their identifications
with Mexico and with Mexican culture. Upon presentation of
the Mexican flag to the association's president by a
representative of the Mexican Consulate, the president
kissed the flag while at the same time expressing his
gratitude for this gift. Furthermore, one politician who
addressed the members exhorted them to "Prove as loyal
to the city of your adoption as you are loyal to your
mother country" thus strongly implying an identification
with Mexico.

In at least the years 1960 and 1961 the Sociedad
Mexicana Azteca placed an announcement in Rumbos de Mexico,
a magazine published under the auspices of the Mexican
Consul General. Both items included a photograph of the
association's officers--now beginning to include members of
the second generation--in formal attire, as well as the
club's salutations to the people of Mexico and the President
of Mexico.[5] In effect, these announcements symbolically
legitimized the existence of the Mexican Aztec Society as a
Mexican association along with reaffirming the ties between
its members and the people of Mexico.

The Mexican Consul General of Philadelphia has
continued to validate the Mexican Aztec Society's symbolic
patriotic function while also utilizing the association in
support of his own professional responsibilities. On the
one hand, in 1937, the consul wrote a letter of praise and
encouragement to the association's general assembly promptly
following the association's initial organization, and in
the following year he formally acknowledged the Mexican

[5]There is reason to doubt that this magazine was
published with regularity.

Aztec Society by attending a banquet which the members held
in his honor.

Varying degrees of patriotic expressions are
reflected the Mexican Aztec Society's meeting minutes. To
illustrate, in 1938, when the effects of the Great Depression were still being felt, the association members made a
monetary contribution toward the Mexican petroleum debt.[6]
Later the members responded to appeals for funds to overcome the devastating effects of an earthquake in Mexico
with an official donation of $10.00 from the treasury as
well as the proceeds of a collection made throughout their
colonia. One also notes, however, that the by-laws
emphatically prohibit any payment of funds to non-members.
In these instances members' feelings of attachment and
obligation to their country of origin over-rode the
restrictions of their association's constitution.

In 1948, the members of the Sociedad Azteca Mexicana
made a collection for a statue honoring the Ninos Heroes.
This was a fund to provide a centennial monument

---

[6]This debt had been incurred as a result of Mexico's
nationalization of her petroleum industry--including the
takeover of several American companies. One wonders to
what extent this nationalization had presented a conflict
of loyalty to the members of the Mexican Aztec Society.

commemorating the youths who defended Chapultepec Castle
in Mexico City against the invading forces of the United
States, sacrificing themselves rather than allowing the
Mexican flag to be captured. However, after the collection
had been taken the officers elected to return the money
rather than sending such a small sum, which would make
them "feel ashamed." Without doubt, the association's
officers had maintained an intense Mexican patriotism which
had not been shared by all other Mexican Americans.

To the Mexican Consul General, the Mexican Aztec
Society afforded an opportunity to reinforce members'
identification with Mexico. Indeed, during World War II
when the United States government, executives of the steel
company, and local residents all urged resident aliens to
become naturalized citizens, the Mexican Consul General
exhorted his compatriots to "remain loyal to their homeland rather than disgracing themselves by accepting the
instruction which led to naturalization." As a substitute
for the naturalization teachings in English, the Mexican
Consul General sent a number of Mexican patriotic materials

to Bethlehem's colonia mexicana in care of the Mexican
Aztec Society. These resources included an illustrated
edition of the Mexican National Hymn, the bulletin
Noticias de Mexico (news from Mexico), and Spanish-
language texts for grades one through three which reportedly
focused upon the Mexican heritage. In response, the
association officers distributed a number of the texts
among Mexican families, retaining the remainder for a
"school" to be held in their meeting room. However, for
want of support from residents of the colonia, this school
never materialized.

Thus, although from the vantage point of the Mexican
Consul, the association provided a source of monetary
donations, a channel for communication with Mexican nationals
in Bethlehem, and a focal point for the relaying of political
propaganda; during recent years, however, only token ceremonial contacts have occurred between the Mexican association and the Mexican Consul General.

In yet another symbolic expression of attachment to
Mexico, delegates representing the association also

established and maintained contacts with members of other
Mexican American associations by attending the annual
Emilio Carranza Memorial Ceremony, an elaborate ritual
honoring a Mexican pilot whose plane crashed in New Jersey
while on a goodwill tour of the United States in 1928.
Commemoration of this event has been a cooperative venture
between a Mexican American voluntary association in
Philadelphia and the American Legion post of Mt. Holly,
New Jersey. Therefore, this observance fostered Mexican
Aztec Society members' interaction with officials of a non-
ethnic voluntary association in addition to manifesting the
symbolic and communication functions associated from this
gathering of Mexican American delegations and representatives of the Mexican Consulate.

Summary

Several functions which researchers have consistently
attributed to voluntary associations located throughout the
world also pertain to the Mexican Aztec Society. This
voluntary association:

1) Provides mutual assistance,

2) "Cushions" the changes imposed upon new migrants
   by providing them with a "cultural bridge,"

3) Socializes members into unaccustomed modes of
   behavior which have recently become appropriate
   for them,

4) Permits members to either intensify or extend
   their social networks,

5) Provides members with opportunities for social
   or economic mobility, and[7]

6) Serves as a source of unity.

Consistent with generalizations about Mexican American
voluntary associations, the Mexican Aztec Society also
provides for:

---

[7]Apparently many Puerto Ricans of Bethlehem view
their social membership in the Mexican Aztec Society as
supplementing their membership in the Puerto Rican association. At regular intervals the Puerto Rican Beneficial
Society, at a cost of several hundred dollars, engages
bands from New York City to play on Saturday nights.
Because most of the local bands performing at the Mexican
Aztec Society compare unfavorably to these New York bands,
on such nights, for lack of Puerto Rican members, the bar
is ill-attended. However, soon after midnight business
begins to boom because many Puerto Ricans make a second
stop at the higher status Mexican voluntary association.
Because of language problems as well as unofficial discrimination, Puerto Ricans are prevented from joining
various local voluntary associations. Therefore, the
Mexican Aztec Society serves a vital function for Puerto
Rican members; it provides Puerto Ricans with an associational opportunity which facilitates contacts with members
of other ethnic groups.

1) Informational and communication networks,

2) Interaction among Mexican Americans,

3) Preservation of Mexican American culture, and

4) A framework for cultural pluralism.

However, the field data cause one to observe that this
association manifests several additional functions more
strongly than it does the preceding functions, which have
been reported in published accounts. As the Mexican Aztec
Society's primary manifest functions, this association
provides for health and bereavement benefits in addition
to striving to foster social integration and a "love for
work." Through the 1950's the Mexican Aztec Society
developed and maintained considerable communication with
Mexican Americans residing elsewhere in the United States.
Despite the fact that this association has always provided
members with health and bereavement benefits, decisions
about the allocation of payments have, nevertheless, also
provided evidence for the Azteca's latent function--social
control of Mexican Americans. As indicated by informants
as well as the Mexican association's minutes, the general

assembly has repeatedly been presented with proposals to
increase the number of services for which members qualify;
however, rarely have the motions to adopt new functions
even been voted upon. For example, children of members
proposed a "Youth Club" and an officer supported the idea
of a credit union, but in both cases the members took no
action. Also, a Mexican American individual, rather than
the Mexican Aztec Society organized El Grupo Mexicano
(a Mexican American children's voluntary association devoted
to Mexican folk dance). Unlike numerous voluntary associations which are organized for the express purpose of
implementing programs for social action, Azteca members
have frequently declined such involvements.

The most salient function of the Mexican Aztec
Society seems to lie in this association's reinforcement of
a prized belief system. By means of Mexican patriotism and
identification with Mexican culture, members manifest the
Mexican Aztec Society's symbolic function which provides
the Mexican association's most important raison d'etre.

CHAPTER V

THE MEXICAN AZTEC SOCIETY: 1970

Preliminary Remarks

Because of disparities in the available sources of data, the present chapter represents a departure from the preceding chapters. In the foregoing, I was largely compelled to rely upon the memories of informants, the association's records, and miscellaneous journalistic descriptions. In as much as utilization of these data bases necessarily limits the aspects of the Mexican Aztec Society's history which can be discussed, the contents of Chapters III and IV reflect the fact that my participant observation encompassed but 2.5 percent of this associa- tion's history (nine months). In contrast, the present chapter--largely the product of participant observation-- describes aspects of Mexican American voluntarism which cannot be obtained from other sources. Rather than strictly confining the points discussed to associational

functions and evidence of formalization, I shall first
discuss the Mexican Aztec Society as a locus for associational activity in order to provide a general orientation
to this association in 1970.

General Description

Facilities

The Mexican Aztec Society's clubhouse consists of a
large, older brick structure of three stories, formerly
used as a furniture store, which is located on Bethlehem's
south side. Due to unrealized plans for business expansion,
both upper floors of the building have lain vacant during
the five years of the association's ownership.

The first floor contains one large open area which
includes a large bar, dance floor, area of chairs and
tables covered with red-checked cloths, billiards area, and
stage in addition to separate rooms for the kitchen, walk-in
cooler, cloakroom, auxiliary bar, office, restrooms, store-
rooms, and foyer. Items of equipment include a color
television set and a jukebox offering both American and

Mexican records. On the walls various members have placed numerous paintings of bullfight scenes, a painting of the restored archeological site of Teotihuacán, photographs of the Presidents of both Mexico and of the United States, a Mexican flag, and several Mexican travel posters. Further-more, a Mexican American photographic technician contributed two six foot square black and white prints of somewhat abstractly treated bullfight scenes. Red letters which spell out "Mexican Club," together with about twelve large red paper balls, decorate the space above the stage. At most times, the interior of the entertainment area is poorly lit, so that none of the decorations, with exception of those over the stage and the abstract bullfight photos catch the eye more than fleetingly. Indeed, the clubhouse reflects a distinctive orientation toward interior decora-tion: whenever an officer of the Mexican Aztec Society judged that his club's decorations were less than perfect, he added additional wall hangings.

The Mexican Aztec Society and the Mexican Club

Once during each month, the voting ("active")
members of the Mexican Aztec Society order to discuss the
general operation of the club as well as association
matters. Social members, although permitted to participate
in the club's activities and use the facilities, neither
possess the right to vote on association business nor the
right to hold office. Because only Mexican Americans and
their spouses are eligible for active membership, the
association's decision making is largely limited to Mexican
Americans. In addition, the board of directors (slate of
officers) meets every Monday night at the clubhouse in
order to deal with the previous week's financial matters
pertaining to operation of the club; various officers
present business reports at the association's regular
monthly club meeting.

Sexual segregation characterizes club-related task
performance. A semi-autonomous, semi-formal group of
approximately twenty female members of the Mexican Aztec

society, the Ladies Auxiliary, convenes at monthly intervals. As its manifest function, the Ladies Auxiliary
exists in order to prepare and serve tacos and enchilladas
to the club's patrons--in keeping with their traditional
sex roles. Furthermore, women have never been elected to
any office save secretary and during but few years have
they held that position. For this reason the female
members have been compelled to depend upon their votes,
their vocal participation, and informal sanctions in order
to influence association decisions. Perusal of the minutes
reveals that women do project a more argumentative image
(perhaps reflecting a bias of male secretaries).

With regard to the club, as distinguished from the
voluntary association, male members emerge yet more firmly
in control of all matters. In addition to administering
the club, male members tend the bar and maintain the
premises as well as constituting nearly all of the patrons
on many nights. With apparent resentment of the verbal
performance of female members, some males say that "the
women talk a lot but they don't come in to work or spend

money very often." Indeed, despite the universal suffrage guaranteed in the by-laws and in the complete name, the Mexican Aztec Society of Both Sexes, the clubhouse remains largely a male bastion.

During 1970 rarely do more than twenty-five members attend a monthly meeting. Generally the meeting convenes in an area near the club's dance floor occupied by tables and chairs, although occasionally a member will say "why don't we stay at the bar so we can get drinks easier?" In the former case, the president sits at a table facing the entire assembly; in the latter case he positions himself in the bartenders' area between the two bars without being able to face the entire assembly simultaneously. Thus, as a result of being situated in a more commanding position, the president tends to be able to direct the proceedings more effectively when the meetings are not held at the bar. The president and assembly usually follow a rudimentary parliamentary procedure in which the secretary and treasurer read reports for approval; old business preceeds new business; and motions are made, seconded, and voted upon.

But, in spite of these attempts at formal structuring, the presiding officer is actually only the first among many discussants, i.e., _primus_ _inter_ _pares_, rather than in firm control of the association's meeting.

Association Activities

The annual cycle of events in the Mexican Aztec Society begins on the first Tuesday of January when, the Board of Directors, the present year's officers take office. Despite lack of attendance in 1970, in April a delegation of association members usually participates in the annual ceremony at Mount Holly, New Jersey which honors a deceased Mexican aviator. On the Saturday closest to May 5, the Mexican Aztec Society holds a banquet in order to celebrate the Mexican defeat of Maximilian's Armies in 1862. During the slack summer period, the association sponsors its "twenty-twenty club"--a series of weekly raffles continuing for twenty weeks. In order to be eligible for each week's drawings, participants must be "paid up" through the current week at the rate of $1.00 per week. On every Wednesday for the duration of the twenty-twenty club, all "paid up" members may potentially win the first "kitty" of the evening, but participating members must be present in order to qualify for the second "kitty."[1] Thus, this system of two prizes encourages association members to congregate at the clubhouse on Wednesdays while also purchasing drinks. Several weeks later, the members celebrate with another banquet the second major Mexican holiday--Mexican Independence on September 16. At the November meetings of the Mexican Aztec Society members nominate officers in preparation for the elections which they hold at the December meeting. Finally, the association members close the annual cycle by hiring an expensive orchestra in celebration of the new year. Because the research was initiated in December 1969, and continued only through August, 1971, the full round of events could not be observed, but the minutes of over thirty years document association activities. Informants report that the celebration of September 16 is much like that of May 5.

During 1970, many of the association's activities focus around the club's sale of alcoholic beverages. From

[1]The "kitty" is a cash prize consisting of a portion of the money collected from members belonging to the twenty-twenty club.

Monday through Thursday, the clubhouse bar is open each evening, but there is no entertainment on these nights. For several years, the association had hired "rock" bands on Friday nights, however, due to declining bar business-- during several unsuccessful months of 1970--performances by these bands have been discontinued. On Saturday night, the entertainment features a local Latin American band, although formerly the association had hired Mexican bands from New York City. The clubhouse doors are opened at noon each Sunday in order to take advantage of the Pennsylvania laws which exempt private clubs from a pro- hibition of Sunday liquor sales. During the evening, another "rock" band completes the Sunday attractions. As for food, an individual member cooks Mexican food Saturdays and the Ladies Auxiliary provides Mexican food on alternate Sundays.

The composition of the club's clientele depends greatly upon the day of the week. On week nights rarely do more than a dozen persons sit at the bar at any one time. Of these several persons, the majority are Mexican

Americans who are over thirty years of age, although a
minority are Puerto Ricans. Few persons of other national
origins frequent the bar during the week, just as few women
visit it on week nights. In contrast, Friday's clientele
is comprised of some Mexican American members and many
persons of other origins, all in their twenties, who come
for "rock" entertainment, as well as the middle aged
members who come in order to work. The Mexican Americans
who patronize the Friday night entertainment seldom
participate in any other activities of the association.
Moreover, they are almost invariably social rather than
active members. On Saturday evening the Latin dance bands
attract Mexican Americans, Puerto Ricans and Cubans,
together with members of highly varied non-hispanic backgrounds. Although Mexican Americans of all ages patronize
the club on Saturday, those in their twenties constitute
the age group least well represented. Moreover, the Puerto
Ricans in the Mexican club on Saturday night often outnumber
the Mexican Americans. Finally, on Sunday, Mexican Americans
over thirty predominate until the "rock" band begins playing

in the evening, when a few young Mexican Americans and
many others in their twenties form the majority of the
patrons.

Few members under thirty participate in the club's
operation. Moreover, although all Mexican Americans over
twenty-one are eligible to become active members, and I
have observed little which indicates that many younger
members of the colonia will become members. In any case,
this lack of participation by young Mexican Americans
suggests that the Mexican Aztec Society's continued
existence is imperiled by ineffective recruitment.

In summary, throughout most weeks of the year,
social members who lack interest in the association's
operation and preservation, provide the bulk of the
patronage enjoyed by the Mexican Aztec Society's clubhouse.
In addition, of the active members, rarely do more than
twenty percent attend the monthly meetings. Furthermore,
less than one dozen devoted members furnish the preponder-
ance of the volunteer labor upon which the functioning of
the association's operations depend. Thus, the physical

operation of the club facilities suffers from lack of
support by the association's voting members--those same
members who have a vested interest in the continuance of
the mutual benefit and sociability functions of the
association.

Within the Commonwealth of Pennsylvania the Sunday
sale of alcoholic beverages is permitted only in private
clubs. Informants insist that formerly a large proportion
of the Mexican American members regularly exercised their
right to drink in "our club" on Sunday. But in 1970, the
right to drink on Sunday is far less important to most
Mexican Americans than it has been previously. Although
the clubhouse doors are opened before noon on Sunday, one
often observes no more customers at any one time during
that afternoon than are observed on any given weekday night
(on other days of the week the club is open only during the
evening). But after the dance band begins playing "rock"
music between 9:00 p.m. and 10:00 p.m., the club may become
crowded with members in their twenties, some of whom are
third generation Mexican Americans. In effect, from the

composition of club patrons on Sunday afternoon and on
Sunday evening, one can infer that the first and second
generation Mexican Americans who run the club are only
moderately interested in its Sunday functions. They
apparently view Sunday instrumentally, as merely a day when
the business is profitable. In other words, those members
who give the bar facility the greatest patronage on Sunday
are persons who are only marginally involved in the
association's operation.

Every day of the week, except Sunday, a pensioned
steelworker living nearby opens the clubhouse doors at
about 7:30 p.m. for the arrival of that evening's bartender. On Monday this "old timer," who has been active
since 1937, also serves as bartender while the board of
directors meet with the society's accountant. Apparently,
though, most members desiring to drink must have satisfied
their desires during Sunday night because on some Mondays
no customers patronize the club, while on other Mondays
only three or four customers appear. Frequently the club
is closed by 10:00 or 11:00 on Mondays.

On Tuesday, Wednesday, and Thursday the club's
business increases slightly in comparison with Monday's
business. Exceptions to this pattern are the one Tuesday
each month when the regular meeting is convened and the one
Thursday each month when members of the Ladies Auxiliary
hold their meeting; this latter event is followed by bridge
games for auxiliary members. Occasionally the association's
dart team uses the clubhouse for a match against another
team on a Wednesday evening. Nevertheless, barring one of
these three, somewhat rare, events which augment the
club's clientele on week nights, there is seldom much
activity at these times.

Evenings "At the Club"

Arriving at the clubhouse at, say, 8:00 p.m., one
frequently observes the presence of only one or two customers. Among those most likely to be sitting at the bar are
Pablo Macías and Miguel Reyes. Reyes, a high school
graduate, is a Puerto Rican steelworker in his forties.
He became an active member before the Mexican American
members voted to restrict subsequent Puerto Rican applicants

to social membership. Somewhat of an entrepreneur, Reyes owns a pool hall near the Puerto Rican club and always flashes a large roll of bills when he is generously buying others drinks. The Mexican Americans involved with operating the bar gratefully acknowledge "That's one guy that spends a lot of money here." Apparently Reyes' membership in social clubs is related to his aspirations for upward social mobility: he belongs to well over a dozen clubs in Bethlehem. Furthermore, Reyes has dated an Anglo schoolteacher for several years; he admits, too, that "I've learned a lot from her." Whether or not Reyes views his participation in the Mexican Aztec Society as enhancing his status, he certainly visits its bar nearly every evening, except when he works on the night shift. Yet he does not participate in the association's monthly meeting when he is present. It is paradoxical that although Reyes loaned the association a substantial sum of money at a time when the officers were refused a comercial loan, he seems to sit at the sidelines as if he were waiting for an invitation to participate in the monthly meetings—an invitation which is never made.

Whenever Miguel Reyes or Pablo Macías is present in the clubhouse as I enter, one or the other is certain to say in the same breath "Buenas noches amigo. Dale un trago" ("Good evening friend." [to the bartender] "Give him a drink."). When I attempted to reciprocate for Reyes' drinks, the Mexican American bartenders sometimes discouraged me from this action, apparently because of the supposed prosperity of Reyes. Being typically short of funds, the problem of reciprocation indeed presented me with something of a dilemma. In the course of the research, Miguel Reyes continued to press drinks upon me for several weeks after which he offered them less frequently having apparently decided that I was sufficiently in his debt. That Reyes perpetuated this imbalance, is indicated by his unchanging response to my purchasing him a drink--within two minutes he reciprocated.

With Pablo Macías the same difficulty developed, except that in his case it is virtually impossible to either refuse or reciprocate his prestations. On the one

hand, verbal refusal of his offered drink usually causes
him merely to order the bartender to place an inverted
class--symbolizing a credit of one drink--upon the bar
rather than serving the drink. On the other hand, an
absolute refusal of his offer offends this sensitive, well-
intentioned "old timer." In the end, I resorted to
reciprocating with gifts to Macías in other domains, for
example, by presenting him with a large photograph of the
house which he had built for himself.

While sitting at the clubhouse bar, members are
less likely to eat "Slim Jims" (sausages frequently con-
sumed in bars and snacks) than they are to eat either
potato chips or chicharones (cracklings) together with hot
chili sauce. The sauce used is less spicy than that served
in Mexico but nevertheless of sufficient potency to bring
discomfort to many unwary "gringos." Other bar activities
include the watching of a color TV, and conversations with
friends; men who do not wish to be disturbed in their
drinking apparently do not frequent the club.

During 1970, "rock" bands performed at the club on
Friday evenings only for a period of approximately five
months. As a consequence, both the number and the composition of the members seen there on Fridays depend upon
whether or not a rock band performs. Whenever live "rock"
is provided, members under thirty predominate, with the
result that one might mistake the evening for a "slow"
Sunday evening. However, members recall that only four or
five years earlier the club often filled to capacity on
Fridays. On Fridays when no rock group plays, the club is
patronized by the weekday "regulars" with the addition of
some members and persons who had come hoping to dance, but
remaining for only one or two drinks. Thus, in 1970,
activity in the clubhouse on Friday nights follows no
single pattern.

On Saturday, the member who has volunteered to
"open up and set up the bar" arrives at approximately
7:00 to 7:30, immediately beginning to stock the beer
coolers, slice lemons, fill the ice buckets, and generally
prepare the bar for the evening's business. If all proceeds

smoothly, other Mexican American bartenders should begin
arriving soon after 9:00 when the patrons also begin
arriving. About this time, the treasurer or some other
active member stations himself at the door in order to
"card" anyone who may not be a "paid-up" member, or a non-
member, or who may be underage. The members expect that in
compensation for their services, which may be required
until 4:00 a.m., these volunteers will serve themselves a
few drinks at the association's expense. In addition, two
or three waitresses, who are seldom all Mexican Americans
receive salaries for their efforts. Furthermore, after
9:00 Juana Reynosa sells tacos, enchilladas, tamales, and
tostadas from the food concession which she runs as an
individual member. After the band ceases playing, Juana
usually divides the remaining Mexican food among the
members who are on duty. Hence, the volunteer bartenders
receive food and a few drinks as compensation for their
efforts.

During the hours of highest activity, 12:00 to 2:00,
at least five bartenders are needed. Generally one of these

men concentrates upon mixing whisky sours, _margaritas_, the potent "drink of the house" called the "bullfighter," and other cocktails. The remaining bartenders serve beer, "seven-sevens," rum cokes, sauterne and soda, and other simple beverages while stationing themselves about the length of the one-hundred-stool bar. In contrast with weeknights, women and couples sit at the bar on Saturday; however most couples sit at the tables which are located on the far side of the dance floor.

Conflict Among Members

As in earlier years Mexican Aztec Society members also conflict with one another while attempting to cooperate in their voluntary association. One particular officer, who appears to owe his office to a dearth of other members' willingness to accept the responsibility, frequently comes under fire from other members who dislike him. Occasionally members complain that "many" Mexican Americans choose not to enter the clubhouse solely because of this one officer's participation. Some persons go so far as to advocate impeachment based upon these subjective

grounds. However, other members quickly observe that the
officer's election was not improper nor do the association's
by-laws contain any provision for impeachment of officers.
Moreover, they emphasize that "we need _every_ member and we
need cooperation--not fighting." Although they are not
always association officers, the persons who most consistently espouse the ideals of rationality, solidarity, and
cooperation are the same members who contribute their
personal time to the many thankless tasks necessary to
operate the club.

The events which led to Pancho Bustamente's resignation from the association provide further illustration of
the organization's latent lines of schism. After one of
the association's two ancient cash registers became
inoperable, the members were jointly faced with the problems
of raising funds for the purchase of a modern machine and
of selecting the particular machine to be purchased.
President Meza authorized Pancho Bustamante to negotiate
the purchase of a replacement, but after Pancho had already
signed an agreement to trade-in the two old machines, and

verbally agreed upon a purchase, several association
officers and active members decided that they should
instead purchase a more expensive model which would perform
additions: thus eliminating some costly errors made by
bartenders. Indeed, discussion at the following monthly
meeting touched upon the ethics and legality of purchasing
a machine from a second company, the value per cost of
both machines as demonstrated by two different salesmen,
and Bustamante's role in the process. Repeatedly Mrs.
Bustamante interjected into the discussion that the members
should not blame her husband, who was absent; invariably,
some other member reassured her that "we're not blaming
Pancho." (Nevertheless, Pancho did take offense that his
delegated responsibility was not honored by the members.)
Eventually the assembled members voted to honor the
existing verbal sales agreement even though the salesman,
as well as the product, of this company made a far less
effective sales presentation than did his competitor.
However, this matter did not end until the following month
when Bustamante accused an officer of accepting a kickback

from the purchase of an inexpensive sign. This officer
replied by charging Pancho with accepting a kickback from
the cash register salesman and since that time Pancho has
never been known to enter the association's clubhouse.

The heterogeneity of Bethlehem's Mexican American
residents also causes conflicts and resentments among
Mexican Aztec Society members. Both second generation
Mexican Americans who married Mexican nationals as well as
their fellow ethnics who married "Americans" assert that
the other Mexican Americans of their age were "like
brothers and sisters to us." To illustrate, if any
"outsider" acted "improperly" with a Mexican American girl,
there was invariably a fight, provided at least one Mexican
American male--often not even related to the female--
witnessed or heard of the impropriety. Furthermore, in the
process of becoming acculturated the second generation
Mexican Americans acquired notions of romantic love, which
in combination with the expressed sentiment, of shared
siblingship effectively obviated the sensual appeal of
other members of their colonia. Apparently these familial

notions were most strong among Mexican Americans who had
lived in the Labor Camp but also occurred with intensity
throughout the Bethlehem colonia. However, Mexican American
females who married members of other nationalities sometimes exclaim, "I wouldn't marry anyone who cated like my
father!" Here the reference is to the absolutism of
paternal authority in the traditional Mexican family, a
notion which numerous second generation Mexican American
females have rejected. As a consequence, they marry men
who are least likely to be rigidly authoratative--i.e.,
males not of Mexican descent. One wonders if the male
Mexican Americans of the second generation did not adopt
the feelings of shared siblingship with females of their
ethnic group as a defensive, face-saving rationalization.
The following evidence for conflict may have resulted from
such factors. While I was tending bar on one Saturday
night, a Mexican-born bartender pointed at three attractive
Mexican Americans saying in English:

> Hey pal, you see those three girls over there?
> They think they're the only beautiful Mexicans
> in the world. They thought they were too good
> to marry Mexicans.

In this particular case I wondered if the informant had not
been rebuffed in his own attentions to one or more of those
women. Because the Latin bands attract to the club Mexican
Americans of great heterogeneity, the gathering, which
constitutes a reunion for some, also exposes intragroup
stresses which are caused by differences in social class
acculturation, group identification, and social prestige.

Lest these illustrations be taken as reason to
condemn Mexican Aztec Society members for divisiveness, one
should note the words of organization theorist Theodore
Caplow: "None of the organizations that have been studied
seems to run smoothly for more than short intervals" (1964:
138). Therefore, the Mexican Aztec Society cannot be
expected to avoid conflict any more than can a business
organization.

Symbolic Function

Each year the Mexican Aztec Society commemorates
the Mexican victory over Maximilian's armies which occurred
at Puebla on May 5, 1862. Celebration of this and Mexican
Independence Day, September 16, constitute the major

Mexican national holidays celebrated at the clubhouse by the members. However, as an indication of declining support for the association, in 1970 the members decided to celebrate only the <u>Cinco</u> <u>de</u> <u>Mayo</u> holiday. During the period in which this festivity was being planned, the chairman in charge of this celebration threatened to resign from the association because he felt that his prerogatives had been usurped by one of the officers. (This officer had independently purchased several decorations for the dance floor.) The conflict was never resolved, but the chairman was finally persuaded to hold his resignation until after May 5. It should be added that the festive event trans-pired after most hasty and cursory planning.

The ceremony began with the national anthems of both the United States and Mexico. Taking into considera-tion the lacks of his fellow clubmembers, the organizer of this celebration had printed for distribution the words of the Mexican national anthem but had made no such provision for the American national anthem. Next in the program the pastor of Holy Infancy Catholic Church gave the invocation

in both English and Spanish. Unlike earlier years when the
association had hired caterers, this year members of the
Ladies Auxiliary prepared and served the meal. Then Alfred
De Los Santos, the officer responsible for contacting the
speakers and guests of honor, initiated the ceremony by
introducing the toastmaster, the solicitor of the Mexican
Aztec Society. After being introduced by the toastmaster,
the president took the floor in order to give the welcoming
address but instead of doing so, he stated that he did not
like to give speeches. Moreover, the president confessed
that "I don't really know exactly what the Cinco de Mayo is,
but I know it's important." Later during the program the
association's president had ample opportunity to learn the
significance of May 5 from the content of the Anglos'
speeches, because to a man they all appeared to have
carefully researched the topic! The various speakers and
guests included the Mexican Consul General and one aide,
an Assemblyman, a Representative, a member of the local
judiciary, and the Assistant District Attorney. Each
politician gave an address in which he, in effect, asked

re-election and promised his support for the exclusive
Sunday sales of liquor in social clubs. They also
invariably sang the praises of one particular officer as a
"Mexican who had received much deserved recognition."
(Apparently the politicians hoped to win Mexican American
support by praising this man. Unfortunately their choice
was poorly made, because, to many Mexican Americans, this
individual may be among the least esteemed of their numbers.)

The remainder of the program for the observance of
the Cinco de Mayo holiday consisted of music by one Latin
orchestra, a performance by El Grupo Mexicano (misspelled
as "Groupo" in the program), and music by a Puerto Rican
orchestra. Although one member of the Latin orchestra is
Mexican, the rhythms played were South American and
Caribbean in origin. Considerable delay was experienced
while each group prepared its equipment. Although the
failure of a record player hindered El Grupo's first
number, the dancers performed dynamic versions of La Culebra
(The Snake), El Baile de los Viejites (The Dance of the Old
Men), and several other traditional Mexican folk dances.

The elaborate costumes worn by the performers either had been purchased by Mexican Americans vacationing in Mexico or had been made by a Mexican American seamstress. Whether purchased or made, the acquisitions of costumes required a considerable investment in either time or money. In addition, during El Grupo's performance there is a great emphasis upon costume; three different sets of costumes were worn during a total time on stage of less than thirty minutes. One wonders whether a function of this elaborate wardrobe is to attract female members to join El Grupo Mexicano. However, the group's adult advisors have been forced to concede to several adolescent notions of fashion in order to make membership attractive: the girls refuse to wear the unstylishly long traditional skirts while the boys feel that it is "queer" to wear baggy white pantaloons.

After El Grupo's performance the Latin orchestra resumed playing dance music and many patrons entered the dance floor. To anyone acquainted with them in other contexts, the men seemed strangely stiff and out of place in their dark suits and ties. Moreover, the elaborate

coiffures, bright satins, glittering brocades, and sequined
laces of the women exceed middle class standards of good
taste. When many people began to leave about 1:00 a.m.,
I realized that the Mexican Americans do not follow the
Latin American custom of dancing until dawn. Nevertheless,
the Mexican Aztec Society's celebration of Mexican
patriotic holidays constitutes this voluntary association's
principal manifestation of its symbolic function.

Member Participation

General Loss of Satisfaction Among Members

As in the past, the Mexican Aztec Society's symbolic
function overshadows each of this voluntary association's
other functions. For example, as expressed by Ann Montoya,
her membership in the Mexican Aztec Society represents far
more than participation in a beneficial society cum night
club. Rather, says Ann, "the club is all we've got." That
is, in Bethlehem the Mexican Aztec Society is the sole
organized manifestation of Mexican American ethnicity. In
her opinion, the meager financial return of $8.00 per week

payable during sickness and the $100.00 paid upon a member's death would alone provide no rationale for active membership if, in addition, the association's cultural orientation were not explicitly Mexican. Without doubt, many other members who value Mexican culture share Ann's perception of the role of the Mexican Aztec Society. However, because this association has not engaged a single Mexican orchestra in several years, members are not attracted to "the club" by a program of Mexican music. Although the bands hired for Latin American Music Night (Saturday) do play some Mexican numbers, as often as not the Musicians are Puerto Rican. Therefore, many Puerto Ricans patronize the Mexican Aztec Society's club on Saturdays, but, as a result of the Mexican American's social distance from Puerto Ricans, only a few Mexican Americans deign to patronize the Puerto Rican association's club. Furthermore, Latin rhythms no longer enjoy the great national popularity which had once attracted many local residents as social members or guests in the Mexican Aztec Society. Also, devotees of "rock" music know that many other social clubs as well as night clubs

in the Lehigh Valley hire superior bands. Members also
acknowledge that they lose additional patronage because
"we don't have the girls"--i.e., singles available for
"pick-ups." Although data are lacking, a decade ago the
Mexican Aztec Society appears to have facilitated member's
mate selection; however no such significant function now
pertains to this association. Partially because of the
prevalent ownership of color televisions and partially as a
consequence of a local decline of interest in social clubs,
many voluntary associations' club operations, in addition
to that of the Mexican Aztec Society, are suffering for
want of patrons.

During the recent years which witnessed the decline
of the Mexican Aztec Society's function as a source of
social prestige for Mexican Americans, Mexican Americans
have also been joining voluntary associations which lack
an ethnic base. Because Mexican Americans are not
systematically denied participation in associations, they
are not compelled to associate only with fellow ethnics.
Therefore, whenever Mexican Americans perceive a reason to

join a special purpose voluntary association--e.g., a
bowling team, P.T.A., or veterans' association--they are
free to enter such organizations. However, in contrast
with cities of the Southwest, none of these special interest
associations are wholly Mexican American. Therefore,
special interests together with the dispersed patterns of
residence and employment have the effect of discouraging
active participation in the Mexican Aztec Society.

Because of the many centrifugal forces which draw
Mexican Americans away from participation in the Mexican
Aztec Society, persons who maintain more than a token social
membership in this voluntary association do so only because
of especially strong personal motivations. In order to
explain why some Mexican Americans do choose to identify
with their association, I shall describe experiences and
attitudes of several such members.

Several Active Participants

Juana Reynosa has the distinction of being the only
female "old timer" who has, for several decades, been a
vocal participant in association matters. Born in Jalisco,

Mexico at the turn of the century, Juana migrated to
Bethlehem in 1923 with her husband and their infant. She
was one of the twenty-nine women and 912 men who founded
Bethlehem's _colonia_ _mexicana_ in that year.

Throughout her forty-seven years of residence in
the United States, Juana Reyosa's fervent Mexican
patriotism has never permitted her to become a citizen of
the United States. Juana's firm belief in the ideals of
the Mexican Revolution has also earned her advocacy for the
revolutionary ideals of Castro's Cuban revolution. Despite
strong ties to the United States, Juana firmly supports
the nationalizations of foreign industries which took
place in both Mexico and Cuba even though many of the
companies seized were American-owned. Juana's opposition
to foreigners who own industrial complexes in Mexico
follows from her resentment that the profits from such
enterprizes should flow out of Mexico without bringing
benefits to the Mexican people. In fact, Juana Reynosa is
an avid supporter of the nationalization of foreign-owned
industries, the Mexican Revolution, and of social revolutions

is general. Juana also strongly supported the Mexican
consul General when he invited the Mexican Aztec Society
to make a monetary contribution toward the debts which
Mexico acquired as a consequence of these nationalizations.

One night at a regular monthly meeting of the
association, Juana Reynosa complained at 8:30 about the
many members who had not yet arrived for their 8:00 session.
Following my suggestion that the members were employing
"Mexican time," Juana replied that the reminder cards which
the active members receive each month should specify "8:00
American time." In effect, this woman, who possesses
considerable Mexican chauvinism, had lost the easy going
view of time common to village Mexico. Thus, although
Juana's emotional ties remain with Mexico, not all of her
attitudes reflect her Mexican origin.

With regard to her own social relationships, Juana
Reynosa subscribes to the attitude that one should depend
upon kinsmen for close relationships rather than depending
upon co-workers or other friends. She says, "I haven't got
any true friends. Just family. It's better that way."

Her orientation has possibly been molded by painful
ruptures of earlier close social bonds of friendship.
Despite Juana's professed orientation, she has sought
rather than avoided social interactions with Mexican
Americans. Reflecting their esteem for Juana, many Azteca
members affectionately know her as "Grammy." Without
doubt, had she chosen to become a naturalized citizen of
the United States, and thus eligible for elective office,
Sra. Reynosa's service to the Mexican Aztec Society would
have been recognized by conferring a leadership status
upon her.

As a member who has for decades faithfully attended
convocations of the Mexican Aztec Society, Sra. Reynosa's
devotion to the association far exceeds that which might
result merely from her control of the Mexican food concession. Because she neither has relinquished her Mexican
citizenship nor her plan to retire to Mexico, her participation as an association member, provides not a "cultural
bridge" or a "refuge" but a temporary partial substitute
for her homeland as well as an expression of her patriotism.

Because Juana Reynosa has always intensely identified with Mexico, her children have maintained a stronger
Mexican identity than most other Mexican Americans of the
second generation. Although many second generation Mexican
Americans intermarried with members of other ethnic groups,
an unusually large proportion of Juana's sons and
daughters married Mexicans or Mexican Americans; two out of
eight children chose Mexicans and two other children chose
Mexican American spouses--a very strong indication of
Mexican orientation. Not surprisingly, several of Juana's
lineal descendants appear among the most active association
members as do several of her affinal kinsmen.

Some persons have called Ann Montoya Juana Reynosa's
most "Mexican" offspring. In fact, Ann sometimes jests that
she went to Mexico in order to find a husband as a response
to the scarcity of eligible Mexican American males. While
residing in Bethlehem, Ann has organized and promoted specifically "Mexican" events for Azteca members. Along with her
sisters Constance and Antonia (the three sisters are in their
middle to late thirties) Ann organized a number of children's

Christmas and Halloween parties at the clubhouse. Thus
during the early 1960's, members' children could attempt to
break ornate Mexican _pinatas_ made for the occasion by an
older member. Then in 1967 Ann became concerned that few
Mexican American children were learning Mexican culture.
Therefore, she organized a traditionally costumed Mexican
folk dance group for Mexican American adolescents.

Possessing the personal abilities which she does,
one can expect that Ann will continue her education,
eventually becoming a professional social worker if not a
social scientist. For several years Ann has worked as a
"neighborhood aid" in a public housing project inhabited
by Puerto Ricans and some others. Having been awarded a
scholarship, she is presently studying evenings toward the
Baccalaureate degree. Although presently lacking formal
training in the discipline, Ann Montoya clearly qualifies
as the sole Mexican American informant who might be deemed
a "natural" social scientist.

Although born in Bethlehem, Ann Montoya partially
validated her identification with Mexico and Mexican

culture by marrying a Mexican national. More than any other local second generation Mexican American she has been disturbed by the assimilation of members of her colonia mexicana. Therefore, she strongly supports the only visible manifestation of Bethlehem's colonia--the Mexican Aztec Society. However, at the same time Ann expresses her personal disgust at the general disaffection which the association's members regularly manifest.

Born in Bethlehem, both Steve and Felipe Meza lived there as infants but then were sent by their father to live in Mexico with their grandmother. Wishing to retain their United States citizenship, they returned to Bethlehem in their early teens after ten years in Mexico. During his high school years in Bethlehem, Steve concentrated upon sports to the exclusion of academics; however these activities resulted in at least one offer of a college athletic scholarship which he declined. Says he, "I could have gone to college, but I don't regret that I didn't go." Instead, Steve enlisted in the Army and after being discharged began to work for a local railroad. Now after

nearly ten years of service, he has "worked his way up to
yardmaster."

At age twenty-nine Steve had been an active member
for only three years when he was elected to a key association office. As an officer he attempts to execute his
office with a firm hand and, whether intentionally or not,
he does so without diplomacy. To illustrate, one of the
club's volunteer workers upon criticism resigned from an
office. Only an hour before the next monthly meeting,
Steve disparaged the volunteer for being so quick to quit
and then, in the presence of the entire assembly, restated
his criticisms to the volunteer.

In these and other respects, Steve appears to be
rather inflexible. For example, of the volunteers tending
the clubhouse bar, the president permits only Steve and his
brother Felipe Meza "close up" (handle the day's receipts).
For this and other reasons, both Steve and Felipe frequently
appear at the clubhouse; they also tend bar there. But if
Steve goes to the association at 11:30, the bar closes by
12:00 unless the business is very brisk. In contrast,

Felipe often modifies his previous plans to close early whenever he observes that a few persons at the bar are "enjoying themselves."

Steve Meza sometimes claims that he reads a great deal, especially about Mexican history. But the literature which Steve reads deals with the sensational exploits of Pancho Villa and Emiliano Zapata. Moreover, Steve in general discounts written histories in favor of the tales told by his father and other "old timers" who served in the Mexican Revolution: "They [the "old timers"] knew what really happened in the Revolution." Steve's father served Villa while still an adolescent and claims to have been paid one peso for each rifle which he could scavenge on the battlefields. Therefore, the father was only exposed to a truncated picture of the battles.

Steve takes great pride in being "Mexican," and, as a corollary, travels to Mexico each year during his vacation. However, Steve is also quick to point out that he goes "everywhere" in Mexico, not merely to expensive hotels in the major cities. He visits the villages and small cities,

purchasing food from steet venders and slipping in cheap
hotels, or so his narrative implies. However, when the
researcher asked how far Steve had traveled on his recent
trip, he replied "all the way," meaning to Mexico City
rather than to Yucatan, Quintana Roo, or Chiapas. Without
doubt, many Mexicans would ill-appreciate the implication
that their nation ceases to exist south of Mexico City.

Although some members praise Steve (as well as
Felipe) Meza as the "member who's keeping the club going,"
one more frequently hears complaints that Steve habitually
ignores the association's past rulings for lack of personal
motivation to learn about these matters. However, much of
the criticism arises because Steve refuses to adopt as a
veneer a large measure of personalism in order to cover his
nakedly utilitarian methods for discharging official duties
as he perceives them. In the course of summarizing his
policies as officer and the consequence of those policies,
Steve states that "I had to clamp down on what a lot of
people were doing and they don't like it." Despite his own
enculturation in Mexico, Steve avoids personalism, instead

preferring to perform his leadership role "by the book."
He treats the Mexican Aztec Society membership body as a
secondary group. On the one hand, members who prefer to
have primary-like social relationships with their officers
feel betrayed by Steve. On the other hand, secure in the
conviction that he has in mind "what's best for the club,"
Steve takes pride in the fact that he is "gonna keep the
club goin' if they like it or not."

Alfred De Los Santos, who has served the association
as an officer during several years, is a second generation
Mexican American in his early thirties. As a child, Alfred
lived in a rural area and his father was rather asocial.
Thus, with only one or two exceptions, Alfred did not know
any Mexican Americans who were not kinsmen. Moreover,
Alfred recalls that his very meagre grasp of English was a
definite handicap in school. In fact, he relates that his
first grade teacher insisted: "You will never get anywhere
if you speak Spanish." Apparently Alfred took this admoni-
tion to heart, if his narrative about his later experience
in the Army is any indication. In the same barracks as

Alfred there was a Chicano. This man made a point of speaking to Alfred in Spanish; but Alfred would always reply in English. After a few weeks of this the Chicano became so infuriated by Alfred's refusal to speak Spanish that he began to beat Alfred, demanding a response in Spanish. Diminutive Alfred took quite a beating until a Negro intervened and threw the Chicano down a stairway.[3]

Consistent with Alfred's apparent avoidance of Mexican culture, he married exogamously with respect to Mexican Americans; however, when in his late twenties Alfred initiated some contact with other Mexican Americans by becoming an active member of the Mexican Aztec Society. Although Alfred's motives for joining the association are obscure, it is known that Alfred promptly became one of the society's officers. Furthermore, his election to the directorate was soon followed by his being appointed representative to the Bethlehem Clubmen's Association. Then, in some manner, Alfred De Los Santos became president of this city-wide association, also being re-elected during the subsequent year. The Clubmen's Association is an

---

[3]Ironically, however, Alfred does not care if his children find spouses within another ethnic group "as long as they don't marry Negroes."

important arena in the informal political process in
Bethlehem. Indeed, very important "contacts" are made by
members of this voluntary association. Thus, in this
respect, the president of the Bethlehem Clubmen's Association holds a somewhat prominent local position. As a
result, De Los Santos may enjoy greater contact with
politicians than almost any other Mexican American.
Because several local politicians have traded upon their
ethnic backgrounds successfully, Alfred's sudden "about-
face" with regard to his "Spanish-speaking" heritage should
not be surprising.

Although Alfred works as a welder, he is oriented
toward some social and economic upward mobility. He briefly
attended a local four year college and now takes night
classes at a nearby community college. Moreover, he
occasionally takes correspondence courses. Apparently,
Alfred has declined to run for political office only
because he suspects that the politico who suggested the
idea to him hopes to win the vote of Spanish-speakers by
means of a candidate who would prove to be manipulable. If

this analysis is correct, the quality of the politician's judgment is deplorable. Alfred's inability and reluctance to speak Spanish is known, and is not likely to win him the "Spanish-speaking vote"; furthermore, although an officer of the Azteca, he is not particularly popular among the members.

In search of a personal identity, Alfred appears to have adopted the Mexican American label only after he realized several years ago that one could benefit from ethnicity. However, even his interactions with Spanish-speaking fellow association members have not stimulated him to revive his long forgotten knowledge of Spanish. Indeed, I have no evidence that Alfred can today speak Spanish, but, nevertheless, it was thought that he could attract Puerto Rican, Mexican, Spanish and Portuguese voters to a political party's ticket.

Although unpopular, Alfred has developed some considerable leadership skills via his experiences as Mexican Aztec Society officer and Bethlehem Clubmen's Association president. Furthermore, the available data lead me to conclude that Alfred has instrumentally employed his association participation as a means to some end, presently this goal is comprehended only by Alfred De Los Santos. He clearly does not labor for the Mexican Aztec Society out of appreciation for Mexican culture, although he may, nevertheless, manifest some ambivalence.

In Bill Diaz's life and personality one discerns compartmentalization of strong Mexican elements and equally strong American elements. Although born in Pennsylvania about forty years ago, Bill has never smoked or accepted liquor in his father's presence: two behavioral indica-tions of the traditional Mexican's respect for one's father. Moreover, when either Bill's father or his older brother makes a statement, Bill will never correct or contradict them. Such is the respect which Bill reserves for his elders, even though he has not lived in his father's house for over twenty years. Even the time at which Bill left his parent's household is consistent with the tradi-tional Mexican family cycle. He set up his own bachelor household soon after his mother died. That is, after the death of his mother, who had mediated between father and children, Bill departed from his father's house and at the same time gained for himself greatly increased personal autonomy: positively valued by the Mexican male.

In Diaz's home, the same deference is expected from his spouse, although the children are permitted to respectfully express more differences of opinion. Concerning household matters, Bill states "when Maria suggests something to me, ninety percent of the time I accept her suggestion with minor modifications, but if I disagree, I say how it should be and the matter is closed." If Bill had married another second generation Mexican American, it is doubtful that his wife would have accepted such a subservient position; however, Senora Diaz was born in a small village in Jalisco, Mexico.

Bill Diaz visits Mexico with his family approximately every two years. During each of these vacations Bill visits his affinal kinsmen in Jalisco. To celebrate the Diaz's visit, their relatives generally wish to go on an outing or picnic. But because Mrs. Diaz's Mexican kinsmen are poor,

Bill always purchases the cases of beer and soda. Moreover, when Bill departs, he leaves the relative $100.00 because "It's a lot to them and not so much to me." Thus, to Bill each vacation to Mexico seems to have functioned to reinforce his self image as an individual deserving of respect.

On one particular trip to Mexico Bill met a mechanic who asked Bill to help him emigrate to the United States. Diaz agreed to do so and toward this end he has, at his own expense, traveled to Harrisburg and Philadelphia, Pennsylvania and even to Guadalajara, Mexico. By 1970, he has expended several hundred dollars for a non-kinsman who was unknown to him two years earlier. I suggest that Bill Diaz has guaranteed himself a large measure of self-respect by establishing this patron-client relationship.

An informant who is not Mexican American but who, nevertheless, knows Bill as a co-worker, has noted that Diaz is constantly making "glowing" statements about Mexico. Indeed, as he states his plans, Bill intends to reside in Mexico as soon as he qualifies for a pension in 1978.

There he will, without doubt, enjoy considerable respect as a "rich" American.

Several years ago, Diaz began part-time work bartending in a bar which caters an upper-middle class clientele after he "got his start [learned the techniques and skills of bartending] at the club." Diaz coordinates this income and his steelworkers salary via a meticulously detailed family financial plan. As an illustration, with some pride Bill points out that "I know exactly how much I am going to spend next week for coffee and donuts. I know that on Saturday night I am going to have South African lobster with my wife at the Hotel Bethlehem's continental Room and I know how much I'm going to tip for that meal." Indeed, in sharp contrast with his definition of family roles, Bill Diaz strives to manage his finances much as he would a business corporation.

Bill presents himself as a primary organizing force among his spouse's many kinsmen. As a case in point, he called a "family meeting" to discuss the situation of a boy in the family who had been graduated from high school

with an A average, but was planning to work for the steel
company. Convinced that the boy possessed a far greater
potential, Bill suggested that the "family" jointly finance
the youth's college education. After obtaining his kinsmen's backing, Bill prepared a detailed statement outlining
their plans which he presented to a loan officer at a local
bank. The official read Bill's statement but then expressed
disbelief that Bill was really a semi-skilled steelworker
(Bill himself has only completed high school). With a
kinsman's house as collateral, the bank official made the
family a loan under Diaz's administration. That is, Bill
disbursed the funds, methodically keeping a complete record
of all transactions conducted during four years. By 1970,
the boy had received his bachelor's degree and repaid the
loan in full.

Apparently Diaz has participated in the Mexican
Aztec Society for as many years as any other second generation Mexican American. For approximately twenty years Bill
has occupied a number of association statuses. At present
Diaz feels that his expenditures of time for the Mexican

club's benefit cause family problems. One evening Bill remarked, "Because of the club, my wife hasn't spoken to me in three days." Nevertheless, Diaz expresses pride in his integrity: "I accepted the responsibility for this office for one year when I was elected, and I won't quit before the end of the term." Informants do, indeed, name Bill as an association member who has "worked hard for the club." Given his professed meticulous attention to detail, systematic organization, and adherence to "the right way to do things," it is consistent that Bill should also criticize the operation of the Mexican Aztec Society maintaining that "The club should be run just like a business. We should know exactly how our finances are every week." Bill insists that he runs his household in a more businesslike manner than the Aztecans administer their incorporated voluntary association.

From his active participation in the Mexican Aztec Society, Bill Diaz derives satisfactions in at least three respects. First, existence of this voluntary association permits him to actively identify with Mexican culture despite continued residence in the United States. Second, to some extent, he also enjoys an honorific status by virtue of his repeated election to leadership statuses. Third, Bill acquires immense personal satisfaction as a result of his services to the association. In his estimation he has selflessly labored for this association. Apparently, Bill finds such returns from his active voluntarism to be indispensable for maintenance of his self-esteem.

About 1900 Pablo Macías was born of poor parents in Jalisco, Mexico. During his youth and young adulthood Pablo worked as a muleskinner. Then in 1926, Pablo departed with his savings, bound for Bethlehem, Pennsylvania.

Upon reaching Bethlehem, Macías found employment in the Bethlehem Steel Corporation Coke Works and also established residence in the company Labor Camp. Pablo resided in the Labor Camp for thirteen years, until the steel company closed the camp. During 1939, the Company official in charge of the camp offered the departing residents the materials in their homes; Pablo was among the Mexicans who utilized these materials to construct a house. For the following two years, Macías labored to complete the construction of his small house, which he proudly veneered with brick.

At approximately the same time that he retired as laborer for the steel corporation, Pablo sold his home because it had begun to require more maintenance than a man his age could provide. Planning to visit Mexico shortly, he sought inexpensive temporary lodgings and moved into a two room apartment on Bethlehem's south side. This unfurnished apartment consists of a bedroom and a kitchen but lacks both bathing facilities and refrigerator. Macías apologizes for the unkempt condition of his apartment, saying that the apartment is now in the same condition that it was when he moved in and that he was not going to clean it for somebody else. Moreover, since Macías sold his house a year or more ago, he has been planning to leave for Mexico "next month"--another reason he spontaneously offers for the condition of his rooms.

In the words of another first generation Mexican American, "Pablo Macias drinks too much nowadays." Apparently Pablo's drinking is related to his being a lonely pensioner who has never married. Pablo's marital status is most important to him because he feels that as a consequence of his being a bachelor, he is "worthless." Pablo occasionally confesses that he wants to find a woman to marry who will say to him "don't you drink ever again." In that case, Pablo insists that he would no longer drink.

After having met and spoken with Pablo once or twice he told me "you know I like everything about you except your beard." Later Pablo accused me of being an F.B.I. agent. At yet another time Macías asked me why I dressed differently. Although other Mexican Americans may have shared some of Pablo's reactions, those informants seldom gave any indication of like sentiments. Without doubt, Macías certainly would not have expressed these feelings except when inebriated. Moreover, Macías suspicions were resolved by the passage of time as he came to know me increasingly well.

When inebriated, Pablo also sometimes confronts me with the statement that "you think you better than other people because you been to school." In all likelihood, Pablo feels inferior because he never learned to read until he arrived in Bethlehem when nearly thirty years of age; while living in the Labor Camp as an adult, another Mexican laborer taught him to read and write. But in spite of Pablo's lack of formal education he continues to make note of vocabulary which he does not understand and either consults a dictionary or asks the patrons at the Azteca bar for explanations.

Pablo Macías remains one of the most colorful and animated of those Mexican Americans who served as informents. To illustrate, one evening Pablo was playfully jesting about his knife (non-existant): "mi cuchillito . . . mi cuchillo . . . mi cuchillote . . . mi machete." In other words, Macías was employing various Spanish suffixes in order to talk about his knives of increasing sizes (non-existant) while feigning an aggressive stance.

One of the association's officers once confided in the researcher saying "Boy! it's hard to refuse a drink from one of those old timers." Apparently no other "old timer" insists so firmly upon proferring drinks than does Pablo Macías. In fact, few persons succeed in reciprocating for the drinks which Macías purchases. However, to insist upon giving Macías a drink also has the effect of encouraging the old man to ignore his medical advice concerning alcohol.

Macías perceives association as constituting a primary group. To this lonely retiree who has been only partly acculturated to American culture, the single most important aspect of this voluntarism lies in the social relationships which his participation permits him to activate with fellow members. Although Pablo's poor health qualifies him for periodic payment of health benefits, he little values this instrumental function of the Mexican Aztec Society. Following the sale of his house, Pablo moved a distance of several miles in order to reside within several blocks of the association clubhouse. For Macías

this voluntary association does clearly serve the function
of refuge: there he can speak Spanish and persuade himself
that Mexican customs are being followed. Because of his
compelling need for satisfying, personal social relationships,
Pablo frequently purchases drinks for other patrons in
attempts to initiate dyadic contracts by means of these
prestations. As I interpret Macías's behavior by providing
more drinks than can be reciprocated, he strives to insure
that members will grant the favor of politely conversing
with him. Because I never rudely insulted him or refused
to speak with him, Pablo valued my friendship despite the
ambivalence which sometimes surfaced after excessive
alcohol consumption. Although some members openly derided
Pablo, most members responded with courtesy. However, some
either refused to accept the prestations or immediately
reciprocated with the consequence of insulting Macías.
So important to Pablo are the social relationships that
obtain among fellow members that he proposes to raise the
membership dues in order to maintain the association's
financial viability. Rather than paying $1.00 per month,

he would agreeably pay as much as $5.00 per month ($60.00 annually); however Pablo fails to comprehend that this move would eliminate many less enthusiastic members and destroy the association for want of participants. In summary, the Mexican Aztec Society provides Pablo Macías with primary social relationships not otherwise available to him.

Roberto Gallego, a member now in his early thirties, was born and resided in Mexico until he immigrated to the United States while in his middle "teens." Presently a steelworker, Roberto explains his status as active, rather than social, member by saying that "you get sickness payments when you're active." Despite several years as an active member, Roberto has yet to be entrusted with an elective office nevertheless, for more than a month in 1970, he has served in the club as volunteer bartender during nearly every evening. Early in my fieldwork, Gallego distinguished himself by an outgoing gregariousness and a propensity to provide "drinks on the house." As one of the few Mexican American members to repeatedly but spontaneously discuss la raza, Roberto by no means intends

to become assimilated to American culture. Instead, he
intends to purchase a ranch in the Valley of Mexico "when
I get rich." Roberto works as a shipping clerk.

Miguel Contreras immigrated from Mexico to the
United States during the 1950's. Like some "old timers" a
generation earlier, he married and then became tied to
Bethlehem by virtue of "the children in school" and
seniority as a steelworker. However, Miguel plans to
return to Mexico as soon as his children are graduated from
high school. He complains that "there's nothing to do in
Bethlehem if you don't want to drink all the time." In
comparison, he idealizes the social opportunities which he
enjoyed as a young man in Guadalajara, Mexico. But because
the "poor are poorer there," he resolves to obtain skills
and knowledge which he can capitalize upon in his homeland.
In his words, "there's more opportunity in Mexico."
Accordingly, he has sent his spouse to beautician school
and encouraged his son to study drafting in high school.
Moreover, Roberto "moonlights" as a general subcontractor
thus availing himself of diverse opportunities for

professional experience. He also admits that he actively
participated in the Mexican Aztec Society in order to gain
administrative experience. In other words, Roberto Gallego
serves the Mexican Aztec Society because of personal
instrumental considerations.

Analysis

The preceding discussion of individuals who con-
tinually participate in Mexican Aztec Society activities
illustrates the factors which motivate a few members to
actively struggle for the maintenance of their voluntary
association. I did not randomly select the eight aforemen-
tioned active members (over one hundred persons pay dues as
active members). Instead, I reasoned that individuals who
have contributed great personal energies as members must
also be the persons for whom this voluntary association
continues to serve a valued function.

As indicated by this sample of active contributors
to association activities, the single most important
function of this voluntary association continues to be

symbolic. Most officers, for example, participate because
they desire a personal identification with Mexico, Mexican
culture, or the Mexican American ethnic group. Other
members who devote considerable time to the association do
so because of sundry motivations related to instrumental
matters such as leadership training, extension of personal
social networks, source of personalistic social relationships, or a "refuge" from less hispanic aspects of
American society. It is also true that members who were
enculturated in Bethlehem are usually less motivated to
sacrifice for the Mexican Aztec Society than are recent
immigrants of Mexican birth.

As a further aspect of the fact that the Mexican
Aztec Society primarily serves to reinforce a prized belief
system--the symbolic function--it is undeniable that affiliation with the association structures but a small portion of
members' lives. Indeed, an observation made by Epstein
about African tribalism pertains equally well to the impact
of this ethnic voluntary association upon its members'
social interactions:

It should be stressed here that tribalism is
always situational; it does not operate
equally or with the same degree of intensity
over the whole field of social relations in
which urban Africans now participate (1961:
104).

Similarly, Frederik Barth observes that:

social systems differ greatly in the extent
to which ethnic identity, as an imperative
status, constrains the person in the variety
of statuses and roles he may assume (1969:
18-19).

The Mexican Aztec Society has but little influence upon

many Mexican American residents of Bethlehem; as for its

Mexican American members who closely identify with the

society, this association's influence upon their lives is

largely restricted to the context of the "club."

This is not to say that the Azteca serves no addi-

tional, although less intense, functions. Many "old-timers"

continue to rely upon this voluntary association's mutual

assistance function even though they may annually enter

the clubhouse only upon rare occasions, if that frequently.

Second generation Mexican Americans also attend association activities in order to socialize with friends whom they would not otherwise encounter. Of course, social members not of Mexican descent patronize the clubhouse largely for reasons of sociability.

CHAPTER VI

SUMMARY AND CONCLUSIONS

<u>Summary</u>

During the years in which Bethlehem's <u>colonia</u>
<u>mexicana</u> was becoming established, the immigrants who
labored for the steel company suffered from underemployment
and a severely depressed wage structure. However, the
steel corporation successfully prevented all effective
unionization until 1941. Therefore, Bethlehem's numerous
immigrants could only rely upon their own ethnic groups for
the mutual assistance which the local economic situation
necessitated. Indeed, many ethnic voluntary associations
were organized in Bethelehem for that express purpose (and
dozens have survived until the present.)

In 1923, Mexicans who founded Bethlehem's <u>colonia</u>
received the industry's lowest wages as entry-level
laborers, and for lack of industrial skills, were relegated
to the most menial and undesirable of jobs. Furthermore,

belief that the Mexicans had been recruited as "scabs" or potential "scabs" compounded with a local distrust of large numbers of males not in the company of their families to produce a situation in which the Mexicans were by no means welcomed to Bethlehem. As responses to these and further exigencies, many Mexicans returned to their home- land during the 1920's while others organized two mutual benefit voluntary associations.

During the Great Depression, approximately half of the Mexicans resided in the Bethlehem Steel Corporation's Labor Camp. Informants state that the camp residents participated in many informal practices which provided for essential mutual aid as well as social solidarity. Further- more, they dwell at length upon the primary group relation- ships which there obtained: intimate knowledge of all other camp inhabitants; integrative fictive, consanguineal, and affinal bonds among co-residents; contexts for satisfy- ing social interactions; and maintenance of social control by means of gossip and ostracism.

As soon as the national economy showed some signs
of recovery in 1937, Bethlehem's Mexicans founded the
Mexican Aztec Society which has survived to the present.
However, except for the association's formative years,
during which the members participated enthusiastically, the
Azteca's continuation remained uncertain until the early
1950's. For more than a decade subsequent to 1937, the
members emphasized associational functions which related
to mutual assistance, Mexican culture, sociability, and
social integration of the colonia mexicana. One should note
that the mutual aid function remained especially important
to members at least until 1941 when the Bethlehem Steel
Corporation recognized the United Steelworkers Union as a
bargaining agent for steelworkers including the Mexicans.

In comparison with the many other groups of
immigrants who have settled in Bethlehem, the Mexicans are
outstanding because of the considerable length of time which
passed before they founded an enduring voluntary association,
fourteen years. The small size of the colonia mexicana
partially accounts for this phenomenon; although 700

Mexican Americans today reside in Bethlehem, as few as 250 may have resided there during the 1930's. Therefore, only with difficulty could Mexicans found and maintain an active voluntary association which recruited only from their own ranks. In contrast, large local populations of immigrants--such as the Wends, Irish, Hungarians, and others--could easily sustain one or more ethnic associations without support from members of other groups. It is of primary importance that the Mexican Aztec Society became "successful" only after its membership body had become ethnically diverse.

Functions Served by the Mexican Aztec Society

During the Mexican Aztec Society's thirty-four year history, members have derived satisfactions from their participation as a result of the voluntary association's functions, both latent and manifest. In search of augmented satisfaction through voluntarism, members have strived to make available further services which, in turn, caused increased formalization once the plans had been implemented.

As a function which all associations must necessarily
incorporate in order to remain viable as organizations, the
Mexican Aztec Society permits members to derive pleasure
from their participation--the expressive function. To
varying degrees this association also (1) provides mutual
assistance, (2) "cushions" the changes imposed upon new
migrants by providing them with a "cultural bridge,"
(3) socializes members into unaccustomed modes of behavior,
(4) permits members to either intensify or extend their
social interactions, (5) provides members with opportunities for social or economic mobility, and (6) serves
as a source of intragroup unity. With the exception of
"providing Mexican Americans with a variety of organizations
to join," each of the functions hypothesized for Mexican
American voluntary associations have been at least weakly
supported by data from the present research. Through
membership in this association, Mexican Americans derive
(1) a context for the dissemination of information,
(2) preservation of Mexican American culture, (3) a framework for cultural pluralism (Alvarez 1971:75), (4) interaction

with fellow ethnics (Treudley 1966:60). As a manifest function members of the Mexican Aztec Society strive to foster social solidarity and a "love for work" in addition to the mutual assistance function already discussed. As latent functions the association also provides for social control of members and communication among colonias. However, the association's general assembly has usually failed to institute additional specialized functions which have been made appropriate by acculturation in the colonia as well as social change in Bethlehem as a whole.

The primary associational function served by the Mexican Aztec Society has always been symbolic. For good reason the lexeme "Mexican" has always survived despite the numerous changes in the association's title which the members have instituted. During the association's first years of existence members emulated earlier immigrants by expressing their patriotic attachments to their country of origin via participation in their own ethnic voluntary association. In recent years this association has provided Mexican American members with a vehicle by which they can manifest their identification with Mexico, Mexican culture, or the Mexican American ethnic group. Indeed, no function save the symbolic continues to provide Mexican Americans with satisfactions not otherwise accessible to them.

Analysis

Like many other joiners, members of the Mexican Aztec Society have learned that they can maintain their association provided that at least a small nucleus of dedicated participants occupy the necessary social statuses, both formal and informal. The Mexican Aztec Society has never counted among its members a majority of the local Mexicans or Mexican Americans who were eligible for admission. (For this reason I do not claim that this dissertation describes Bethlehem's colonia mexicana per se.) Indeed, the association appears to have entered a period of semi-dormancy while its members were otherwise occupied with the war mobilization of the 1940's. Only during several years when this voluntary association was enjoying great financial prosperity and immense popularity among nearly all local social groups, did many Mexican Americans

begin to participate in their voluntary association with
detectable enthusiasm.

I contend that for less than one decade out of the
more than three decades of existence the Mexican Aztec
Society fulfilled several functions which it had never
provided before and which it, in all probability, never
will provide again. This is because to Mexican Americans
of Bethlehem, their voluntary association's achievements of
the 1950's represent a symbolic rite of passage: an ethnic
group which had been despised in the 1920's had, within one
generation, far progressed toward economic and social
mobility. The association's permanent rental of a clubhouse, incorporation as a nonprofit organization, and
receipt of a liquor license all establish that Mexican
Americans had achieved respectability and acceptance
approximately on a par with others of Bethlehem's numerous
ethnic groups. Indeed, this interpretation is supported
by the local populace's unhesitant response to the creation
of a specific social status for persons who seek sociability
within the Mexican Aztec Society; thousands joined. One

does not, of course, rush to participate in a voluntary association which is run by lepers, untouchables, or members of other despised groups. Therefore, the Mexican Aztec Society's enormous growth during the 1950's yields evidence that by that time period the Mexican Americans of Bethlehem had, as one man said, "made it."

Without doubt, the association's expansion also depended upon the attractions offered by membership. Indeed, in 1955 the soon-to-become nationally popular Latin American musician Prez Prado indirectly stimulated local interest in the Mexican Aztec Society when his recording of "Cherry Pink and Apple Blossom White" sold over one million records. Both this "hit record" and "Patricia," which he released in 1958, helped to make the cha cha, a dance step, immensely popular in Bethlehem. Indeed, many Bethlehem residents referred to the Mexican Aztec Society as the "Cha Cha Club." This association's membership body expanded further as a consequence of this image and the popularity of Latin rhythms.

Furthermore, the Mexican Aztec Society of the
1950's provided Mexican American members with some opportunity to achieve additional social and economic mobility.
It enabled individual Mexican Americans to enhance their
own prestige by becoming of importance in the "Cha Cha
Club." They could learn occupational skills, make useful
contacts with influential local citizens, and proudly
extend invitations to visit "our club." No longer did
Mexican Americans solely interact with working class steel
company employees. At the clubhouse they encountered
fellow members of all social classes, including the
wealthy owner of a large local department store. Indeed,
at that time, Mexican Americans comprised the minority of
the association's social members. Furthermore, via this
association the colonia mexicana created channels of communication with educational, political, charitable, and
other institutions in the Lehigh Valley. To some extent,
other residents of Bethlehem thrust upon the Mexican
association the function of intermediary between colonia
and other groups. Indeed, this assumption reflects a

tendency to consider ethnic club officers as spokesmen for
the ethnic groups which they represent. Accordingly, local
politicians continue to rely upon ethnic clubs as a readily
mobilizable source of electoral support.

Today Mexican Aztec Society members idealize their
voluntary association of some twenty years past. However,
barring an influx of thousands of Mexican immigrants within
an interval of a few years, it is highly improbable that
Bethlehem's colonia mexicana will ever again experience
this "Golden Age." Moreover, unless some unanticipated
spark ignites a "Chicano consciousness" in Bethlehem,
assimilation of Mexican Americans into the general population appears immensely more probable. In light of these
factors, one should reconsider attitudes voiced independently
by several informants to the effect that "you should have
studied the colonia back in the "fifties." This was not
merely a period when the colonia was more integrated and
less acculturated; for the Mexican Aztec Society it was an
idealized era of fluorescence which presaged the decline
that followed.

The Mexican Azteca Society's expansion foretold
its decline. Through their participation as members in the
1950's, Mexican Americans initiated social relationships
with a highly heterogeneous group of fellow members.
These contacts, in turn, led Mexican Americans into new
activities, including participation in non-ethnic voluntary
associations. Although the association's successes
initially appeared to mobilize and draw the colonia mexicana
inward, via centripetal forces, associational growth
actually activated numerous centrifugal forces which led to
the association's present scarcity of dedicated members and
of manpower. Mexican Americans now enjoy other activities
which they perceive to be more vital to their individual
interests than active participation in the Mexican Aztec
Society.

As for the Bethlehem residents who formerly filled
the clubhouse to capacity, the Mexican atmosphere lost its
novelty, Latin rhythms diminished in popularity, television
transformed American patterns of entertainment, and participation in ethnic voluntary associations generally lost some

local appeal. Concomitantly, fewer non-hispanic persons
patronized the clubhouse, "our club" also began to hold
fewer attractions to Mexican Americans. The addition of
"outsiders" necessarily added an element of impersonality
to the interactions among members of a group which in many
respects had never previously resembled a primary group.
Despite exceptions, in recent years the numbers of
"dedicated" participants in the Mexican Aztec Society have
become decimated. Furthermore, few members continue to
value participation in their association except those who
appreciate the association's symbolic function. However,
if the members choose to retrench by obtaining a less
expensive clubhouse, which also would require fewer man-
hours for its operation, they can preserve their association
indefinitely or at least as long as they can depend upon
the efforts of a core of ten or so members.

    For most participants today the Mexican Aztec
Society satisfies a symbolic function; however some members
relate to fellow members as if they constitute a primary
group while other members relate to fellow members as if

they constitute a secondary group. This observation accounts for much of the conflict which characterizes the association's membership body. To illustrate, officers who apply starkly utilitarian methods in the performance of their leadership roles usually incur resentment of the members who believe that warm social relationships among participants should take precedence over impersonal considerations of efficiency. In other words, members of the first sort relate to fellow members via secondary relationships; members of the second sort relate to fellow members via primary relationships; and strife results from these contrasting expectations.

In summary, the Mexican Aztec Society's fundamental function has always been this association's symbolic manifestation of affiliation with Mexico. However, because of an accident of history, the members achieved full status for their association at approximately the same time that certain aspects of Latin culture began to enjoy immense popularity in the United States. At that time, the Mexican Aztec Society rapidly expanded both its capital resources and its membership body; nonetheless this growth resulted less from support by Mexican Americans than from support by members of other ethnic groups. Indeed, members collectively departed from their association's primary function (symbolic), instead creating a large and commercialized night club. Because the commercialization represented a deemphasis of far more enduring bases for association—such as identification with Mexican culture, it is these primary functions that have survived the association's decline. In contrast with most other ethnic voluntary associations in Bethlehem, the Mexican Aztec Society did not prosper largely because of support from within their ethnic group. Dependence upon the patronage of members not of Mexican descent inevitably subjects the Mexican Aztec Society to the vicissitudes of fadism and other forms of shifting popularity.

Formalization of Ethnic Voluntary Associations

Except for the fact that the Mexican Aztec Society has never attained several of the later stages of formalization, the Tsouderos model has been shown to provide good descriptive adequacy. The Mexican Americans of Bethlehem did, indeed, progress from informal voluntary association to increasingly formalized association: there was increased differentiation among membership statuses, growth in the membership body, attenuation of intragroup communication, decline of primary social relationships, and a general disaffection among members to describe but a few aspects. In other words, the constituent processes which Tsouderso delineates do illuminate this association's development. As an explanation of the observed discrepancies, however, I suggest that the Mexican Aztec Society has diverged from the Tsouderos model both as a consequence of its ethnic affiliation and exogenous variables specific to Bethlehem, Pennsylvania.

Barring an increase in number of members, voluntary associations do not usually manifest extensive formalization. For example, few informal voluntary associations of a small group of friends need a formal set of by-laws in order to facilitate their cooperative efforts, but as the membership

becomes enlarged, formalization becomes increasingly
probable if not necessary. Also, barring an influx of new
members, most small associations would find it unfeasible
to contemplate segmentation into two or more branch
associations; such fission multiplies the total number of
active participants which are essential to the organization's
continuation and therefore may require the services of more
devoted members than exist. At the stage of formalization
in which a central agency controls a network of local
associations, leaders discharge their administrative duties
either without renumeration or with payment for part-time
work. Only when the administrative tasks become excessive
and only when the association's resources permit, do
members institute the status of professional executive.
Unless the membership body has grown, the administrative
work load and the organization's resources are not likely
to both necessitate and also permit the formalization which
the payment of one or more full-time salaries indicates.

Because of insufficient recruitment of members, the
Mexican Aztec Society has not experienced the growth which

is prerequisite to Tsouderos's later stages of formalization (3 through 5). But in his own research Tsouderos purposely elected to investigate voluntary associations which had already become centrally organized networks of local constituent associations. Should the Mexican Aztec Society experience considerable cumulative growth, in all likelihood a far greater portion of the Tsouderos model would then pertain to this association. As the first step toward formulating preliminary notions about the formalization of ethnic voluntary associations, I shall discuss factors which either have prevented or permitted formalization of the Mexican Aztec Society.

Because fewer than one thousand Mexicans or Mexican Americans have ever resided in Bethlehem simultaneously, this social group's potential for mono-ethnic voluntarism accordingly suffers. In comparison, local ethnic groups such as the Italians, Irish, Hungarians, Wends, Ukranians, and others, each of which number several thousand or more, have had considerably less difficulty in recruitment of members. This observation leads to the hypothesis that the

likelihood of formalization in ethnic voluntary associations
increases in direct proportion to the size of the ethnic
group.

Following Frederik Barth, who employs the concept
of ethnicity as one of the bases for organized social
interactions among individuals and groups of individuals
(1969:10), I observe that members of explicitly ethnic
voluntary associations, almost by definition, agree--whether
happily or unhappily--to be treated by members of the other
groups in those ways which are deemed appropriate to their
particular ethnic identifications. By joining a predominantly Mexican American voluntary association, Mexican
Americans agree to be identified and treated as Mexican
Americans. Indeed, in some localities ethnics elect to
join ethnic associations because they have been denied
either admission to, or some of the rights of, membership
in the associations which are controlled by more powerful
groups. Therefore, I hypothesize that lack of accessibility
to other associations increases the likelihood that members

of an ethnic group will participate in those associations
which fellow-ethnics control.

Residents of Bethlehem assume that members of
ethnic groups will utilize participation in ethnic
voluntary associations as a vehicle for both the expression
of identification with their cultural heritage and the
manifestation of their ethnicity. However, one would
anticipate that somewhat fewer members of ethnic groups
would participate in ethnic voluntary associations if their
fellow residents either did not expect or did not permit
the existence of such associations. Taken to the logical
extreme, ethnic voluntary associations could attain but
little formalization if formal voluntarism were prohibited.
Without doubt, local attitudes about ethnic voluntarism do
influence the formalization of ethnic voluntary associations
by either encouraging or discouraging participation.

Receptivity of members of dominant groups to the
cultural heritage of an ethnic group may potentially
strengthen the development of voluntarism within ethnic
groups such as Mexican Americans. Perched atop the cha cha

bandwagon, during the 1950's the Mexican Aztec Society admitted thousands of applicants for social membership thus accepting extensive social and financial support from individuals of diverse origin. Because Mexican American social members constituted but a small minority of the social members, it is reasonable to infer that had the membership body been limited to Mexican Americans, the Mexican Aztec Society would not have achieved the formalization which did occur. Hence, the presence of multi-ethnic support for an ethnic voluntary association may augment that organization's growth and formalization just as the absence of external support may hamper growth and formalization.

The Mexican Aztec Society lost members because some of the functions which it had once usefully provided for participants became more readily satisfied elsewhere. Furthermore, this association neglected to expand its services in order to capitalize upon needs which its members have but recently perceived. As organizations designed to further the special interests of members,

voluntary associations must continue to benefit the participants. Despite the fact that the voluntary associations
are ubiquitous in the United States as well as other
societies, particular voluntary associations are among the
most fragile of all social institutions; they disappear as
soon as the members cease to perceive that benefits are to
be derived from participation. In this respect ethnic
voluntary associations are like other types of associations.
The continued formalization of ethnic voluntary associations
is contingent upon ability to provide functions which the
members desire (cf. Green 1969; Kenny 1961; 1962).

Without doubt, had Bethlehem continuously remained
a destination for Mexicans migrating to the United States,
then a far larger number of individuals would always have
resided there who could have derived satisfaction from
participating in the Mexican Aztec Society. Also, following the cessation of other migrations, Kenny (1961; 1962),
Green (1969) and others note the declines of those ethnic
voluntary associations which serve recent immigrants. In
societies where immigrants become rapidly acculturated, if

not also assimilated, continued formalization of ethnic voluntary associations may be contingent upon the continuing immigration of those ethnic groups. As a related observation, the assimilation of ethnic groups by the dominant groups precludes increased formalization in ethnic voluntary associations if not also threatening the existence of such associations. These statements depend upon the truism that ethnic associations cannot survive the demise of ethnic groups. Furthermore, ethnic groups are perpetuated whenever the net flow of individuals across the ethnic boundary is either positive or zero (Barth 1969). For example, the rate of immigration would equal or exceed the rate of assimilation in this case. Therefore, the variables of immigration and assimilation also have an impact upon the possibility of formalization in ethnic voluntary associations.

Lest this analysis of one particular Mexican American voluntary association be taken as an assertion that all ethnic associations or all Mexican American associations manifest as little formalization as has the

Mexican Aztec Society, I hasten to explain that numerous
highly formalized ethnic associations presently have state-
wide if not national bases. As I have discussed elsewhere
(vide Chapter I), Mexican Americans have organized LULAC,
the American GI Forum, and other voluntary associations
which exemplify Tsouderos's stages of greatest formalization. Jews have formed international association B'nai
B'rith, Negroes the national association NAACP, Italians
the United Italian American League, and so on. In other
words, many ethnic voluntary associations either have or
will manifest far more formalization than has the Mexican
Aztec Society.

Based upon the "melting pot" theory of assimilation,
one anticipates the disappearance of ethnic minorities so
that the need for formalization in ethnic voluntary
associations becomes obviated. However, in this era of
group pride and consciousness raising on the part of many
social groups, "Europe's millions" who reside in the
United States have refused to fulfill the melting pot
prophesy. Therefore, one cannot predict the cessation of

formalization in ethnic voluntary associations because of
the melting pot phenomenon.

Because of the intensive and extensive influences
which other social groups exercise upon ethnic populations,
no model which is said to describe the changes that occur
within ethnic voluntary associations can do so without
taking into consideration a constellation of factors which
influence the viability of such associations: size of
ethnic population (both local and aggregate), accessibility
of other voluntary associations, local attitudes toward
voluntarism, continuance of ethnic populations, local
attitudes toward particular foreign cultures, and services
rendered by ethnic voluntary associations to members. By
appending these considerations to the Tsouderos model, the
composite model enjoys enhanced pertinency to the changes
which occur in ethnic voluntary associations.

I have intentionally discussed the formalization of
ethnic voluntary associations rather than more narrowly
focusing upon Mexican American associations. Despite the
fact that these tentative extensions of Tsouderos's model

can be stated more confidently for the United States than
for the entire universe of modern state level societies,
this reformulation pertains as well to other ethnic groups
as it does to Mexican Americans.

Implications for Mexican American Voluntarism

Although study of a single Mexican American
voluntary association can by no means determine the
voluntarism patterns of all Mexican Americans, this
research can, nevertheless, disprove some erroneous notions
about the ethnic group which comprises the nation's second
largest minority. To begin, the rate of Mexican American
participation in this particular association equals or
surpasses the national average of joining in the United
States. Also, this research has yet to uncover any support
for the belief that Mexican American culture is maladaptive.
In Bethlehem few Mexican Americans are poor, and, moreover,
members such as Ann Montoya successfully achieve social and
economic mobility while preserving a cultural pluralism.
As disproval of yet another popularly held misconception

about Mexican American voluntarism, this dissertation
demonstrates that, despite internal conflict, the members
have been able to provide the requisite leadership for the
maintenance of their association. If ever the issue
demanded additional data, through their participations in
the Mexican Aztec Society the members have effectively
demonstrated that Mexican Americans can organize themselves.

Nevertheless, these conclusions must be taken as
tentative because the Mexican Aztec Society may well be
atypical of Mexican American voluntary associations.
Additional studies of Mexican American voluntary associations must be undertaken in order to determine whether the
present findings can be extended to other colonias. I
know of only two other studies which employed the requisite
participant observation: Samora's doctoral dissertation
(1953) which provided little data for the several associations which he examined and Rynearson's as yet uncompleted
doctoral dissertation (personal communication). Because of
the scarcity of comparable investigations further intensive
participant observation in various colonias is necessary

before one can determine which, if any, attributes of
Mexican American voluntarism are uniquely <u>Mexican</u> <u>American</u>
and which can be generalized to all of the Mexican
American population.

BIBLIOGRAPHY

1970 Census of Population: General Social and Economic
Characteristics. Pennsylvania. Washington: United
States Department of Commerce.

Alvarez, Salvador.
1971 Mexican-American Community Organizations. El
Grito 4:68-77.

Amsbury, Clifton
1972 Reply to Anderson's "Voluntary Associations in
History." American Anthropologist 74:770.

Anderson, Robert T.
1966 Rotating Credit Associations in India. Economic
Development and Cultural Change 14:334-339.
1971 Voluntary Associations in History. American
Anthropologist 73:209-222.

Anderson, Robert T., and Gallatin Anderson
1958 Voluntary Associations and Urbanization. American
Journal of Sociology 65:265-273.
1962 The Indirect Social Structure of European Village
Communities. American Anthropologist 64:1016-1027.

Arensberg, Conrad M., and Solon T. Kimball
1965 Culture and Community. New York: Harcourt, Brace
and World, Inc.

Arnold, Charles August
1928 The Folk-lore, Manners, and Customs of the Mexicans
in San Antonio, Texas. Master's Thesis, University of
Texas.

329

Arsenian, Seth, and Arthur Blumberg
    1966 Volunteers in the Y.M.C.A. The Government of
    Associations: Selections from the Behavioral
    Sciences. William A. Glaser and David L. Sills, eds.
    Totowa, N.J.: The Bedminster Press, Inc.

Babchuk, Nicholas and C. Wayne Gordon
    1962 The Voluntary Association in the Slum. University
    of Nebraska Studies, New Series No. 27. Lincoln, Neb.:
    The University of Nebraska.

Babchuk, Nicholas, and Charles K. Warriner
    1965 Introduction. Sociological Inquiry 35:135-137.

Babchuk, Nicholas, and John N. Edwards
    1965 Voluntary Associations and the Integration
    Hypothesis. Sociological Inquiry 35:149-162.

Banton, Michael
    1956 Adaptation and Integration in the Social System of
    Temne Immigrants in Freetown. Africa 26:354-368.
    1957 West African City: A Study of Tribal Life in
    Freetown. London: Oxford University Press.
    1968 Voluntary Associations: Anthropological Aspects.
    International Encyclopedia of the Social Sciences, XVI.
    D.L. Sills, ed. New York: Macmillan.

Barber, Bernard
    1965 Participation and Mass Apathy in Associations. In
    Studies in Leadership: Leadership and Democratic
    Action. Alvin W. Gouldner, ed. New York: Russell and
    Russell, Inc.

Barbosa-Dasilva, J.F.
    1968 Participation of Mexican-Americans in Voluntary
    Associations. University of Notre Dame, Social Science
    Training Laboratory, Research Reports in the Social
    Sciences. Vol. 2.

Barbour, Henry Ogden
1968   Private Club Administration. Washington, D.C.:
    Club Managers Association of America.

Barnes, J.A.
1972   Social Networks. Addison-Wesley Modular
    Publication No. 26. Reading, Mass.: Addison-Wesley
    Publishing Co.

Barth, Frederik
1969   Ethnic Groups and Boundaries: The Social
    Organization of Culture Differences. Boston: Little,
    Brown and Co.

Baskauskas, Luicija
1971   An Urban Enclave: Lithuanian Refugees in Los
    Angeles. Unpublished Ph.D. Dissertation, University
    of California at Los Angeles.

Beard, Charles and Mary Beard
1930   The Rise of American Civilization. New York:
    Macmillan.

Berreman, Gerald D.
1971   Self, Situation and Escape from Stigmatized Ethnic
    Identity. New York: Paper presented at the 70th
    meeting of the American Anthropological Association.

Bethlehem Globe-Times
    a   "Shortage of All Kinds of Labor Shown in Report,"
        March 21, 1923, p. 5; "State Notes," March 21, 1923,
        p. 5.
    b   "More Mexicans Arrive," April 26, 1923, p. 6.
    c   "Mexicans Asked to Move," April 11, 1923, p. 12.
    d   "Fire in Mexican Colony," June 21, 1923, p. 6.
    e   "Stabbed in Fight," August 29, 1923, p. 9.
    f   "Can't Find Bad Mexican," December 24, 1924, p. 1;
        "A Costly Celebration," January 1, 1925, p. 1.

g "Local Police Raid Gambling House," December 22, 1926,
   p. 11.
h "Drunken Mexican Goes on Rampage with Gun,"
   September 17, 1926, p. 11 [names deleted].
i "Mexican Colony to Hold Dance Tonight," September 15,
   1926, p. 21.
j "Northampton Heights," February 18, 1924, p. 4.
k "Mexico Little Leaguers Limp into Bethlehem,"
   August 13, 1963 [clipping, n.p.].
l "Area Residents Celebrate Mexican Independence Day,"
   September 23, 1968, n.p.
m "Steel Mills 'Imported' Mexicans as Laborers,"
   [1966], n.p.

Boskin, Leonard
   1969 Urban Racial Violence in the Twentieth Century.
   Beverly Hills, Calif.: Glencoe Press.

Bott, Elizabeth
   1968 Family and Social Network: Roles, Norms, and
   External Relationships in Ordinary Urban Families.
   London: Tavistock Publications.

Brandel-Syrier, Mia
   1971 Reeftown Elite: A Study of Social Mobility in a
   Modern African Community on the Reef. London:
   Routledge and Kegan, Paul.

Briegel, Kaye
   1970 The Development of Mexican-American Organizations.
   In The Mexican-Americans: An Awakening Minority.
   Manuel P. Servin, ed. Beverly Hills: Glencoe Press.

Brody, Eugene, ed.
   1970 Behavior in New Environments: Adaptation of
   Migrant Populations. Beverly Hills: Sage
   Publication.

Broom, Leonard, and John I. Kitsuse
  1955 The Validation of Acculturation: A Condition to
    Ethnic Assimilation. American Anthropologist
    57:44-48.

Brown, D.E.
  1973 Voluntary Association: A Further Comment.
    American Anthropologist 75:309-310.

Burma, John H., ed.
  1970 Mexican-Americans in the United States: A Reader.
    Cambridge, Mass.: Schenkman Publishing Co., Inc.

Caplow, Theodore
  1964 Principles of Organization. New York: Harcourt,
    Brace & World, Inc.

Carrasco, Pedro
  1961 The Civil-Religious Hierarch in Mesoamerican
    Communities: Pre-Spanish Background and Colonial
    Development. American Anthropologist 63:483-497.

Casavantes, Edward
  1971 Pride and Prejudice: A Mexican American Dilema.
    In Chicanos: Social and Psychological Perspectives.
    Nathaniel N. Wagner and Marsha J. Haug, eds. Saint
    Louis: The C.V. Mosby Co.

Chapin, F. Stuart, and John E. Tsouderos
  1955 Formalization Observed in Ten Voluntary
    Associations: Concepts, Morphology, Process.
    Social Forces 33:306-309.

Chavez, Cesar
  1971 The Organizer's Tale. In The Chicanos: Mexican
    American Voices. Ed Ludwig and James Santibanez, eds.
    Baltimore: Penguin Books Inc.

Clark, Margaret
   1970 Health in the Mexican-American Culture: A
   Community Study. Berkeley: University of California
   Press.

Comhaire, Sylvia
   1950 Associations on the Basis of Origin in Lagos,
   Nigeris. American Catholic Sociological Review
   11:234-236.

Cuyas, Arturo
   1966 Appleton's New Cuyas English-Spanish and Spanish-
   English Dictionary. New York: Appleton-Century-
   Crofts.

Daday, Rt. Rev. Msgr, Stephen J.
   1966 Chronicle of the Catholic People in Bethlehem.
   Bethlehem, Pennsylvania [pamphlet apparently reprinted
   from newspaper article].

Davis, Ethelyn Clara
   1936 Little Mexico: A Study of Horizontal and Vertical
   Mobility. Unpublished Masters Thesis, Southern
   Methodist University.

Diaz-Guerrero, Rogelio
        Mexican Assumptions about Interpersonal Relations.
   Etcetera 16:185-188.

Divine, Robert A.
   1957 American Immigration Policy: 1924-1952. New Haven:
   Yale University Press.

Dotson, Floyd
   1965 A Note on Participation in Voluntary Associations in
   a Mexican City. In Readings in Contemporary Latin
   American Culture. New York: Selected Academic Readings,
   Inc.

Doughty, Paul L.
   1969 La Cultura del Regionalismo en la Vida de Lima,
         Peru. America Indigena 29:949-981.
   1970 Behind the Back of the City: "Provincial" Life in
         Lima, Peru. In Peasants and Cities: Readings in the
         Anthropology of Urbanization. William Mangin, ed.
         Boston: Houghton, Mifflin Co.

Eidheim, Harald
   1969 When Ethnic Identity is a Social Stigma. In
         Ethnic Groups and Boundaries: The Social Organization
         of Cultural Difference. Frederik Barth, ed. Boston:
         Little, Brown and Co.

Eisenstadt, S.N.
   1961 The Social Condition of the Development of
         Voluntary Association--A Case Study of Israel.
         Scripta Hierosolymitana 3:104-125.

Eislein, E.B.
   1958 Voluntary Associations in European Communities.
         Unpublished M.A. Thesis, University of Arizona.

Epstein, A.L.
   1969 The Network and Urban Social Organization. In
         Social Networks in Urban Situations: Analyses of
         Personal Relationships in Central African Towns.
         J. Clyde Mitchell, ed. Manchester: Manchester
         University Press.

Fabian, Ilona
   1971 Immigration: Cognitive Dislocation and the Problem
         of Historical Continuity. Paper presented at the 70th
         meeting of the American Anthropological Association,
         New York.

Fabrega, Horacio, Jr.
    1970 Mexican-Americans of Texas: Some Social
    Psychiatric Features. In Behavior in New Environments:
    Adaptation of Migrant Populations. Eugene B. Brody,
    ed. Beverly Hills: Sage Publications.

Federal Writers' Project. Work Projects Administration.
    1939 Northampton County Guide. Bethlehem, Pa.: Times
    Publishing Co.

Felter, Eunice
    1941 The Social Adaptations of the Mexican Churches in
    the Chicago Area. Unpublished M.A. Thesis, University
    of Chicago.

Foster, George M.
    1948 Empire's Children: The People of Tzintzuntzan.
    Mexico City: Smithsonian Institution, Institute of
    Social Anthropology, Publication No. 6.
    1961 The Dyadic Contract: A Model for the Social
    Structure of a Mexican Peasant Village. American
    Anthropologist 63:1173-1192.
    1963 The Dyadic Contract in Tzintzuntzan II: Patron-
    Client Relationship. American Anthropologist
    65:1280-1294.
    1967 Tzintzuntzan: Mexican Peasants in a Changing
    World. Boston: Little, Brown and Co.

Frankenberg, Ronald
    1957 Village on the Border: A Social Study of Religion,
    Politics, and Football in a North Wales Community.
    London: Cohen & West.

Freedman, Maurice
    1967 Immigrants and Associations: Chinese in Nineteenth
    Century Singapore. In Immigrants and Association.
    Lloyd A. Fallers, ed. The Hague: Mouton.

Freilich, Morris, ed.
 1970   Marginal Natives: Anthropologists at Work.
 New York: Harper & Row, Publishers.

Fromm, Erich, and Michael Maccoby
 1970   Social Character in a Mexican Village: A
 Sociopsychoanalytic Study. Englewood Cliffs, N.J.:
 Prentice-Hall, Inc.

Galarza, Ernesto
 1970   Spiders in the House and Workers in the Field.
 Notre Dame: University of Notre Dame Press.
 1971   Barrio Boy. Notre Dame: University of Notre
 Dame Press.

Gallagher, Orvoell R.
 1966   France. In The Government of Associations:
 Selections from the Behavioral Sciences. William A.
 Glaser and David L. Sills, eds. Totawa, N.J.: The
 Bedminster Press, Inc.

Gamio, Manuel
 1930   Quantitative Estimate: Sources and Distribution of
 Mexican Immigration into the United States. Mexico
 City: Talleres Graphicos.
 1969a   Mexican Immigration to the United States. New
 York: The Arno Press and the New York Times.
 1969b   The Mexican Immigrant: His Life Story. New York:
 Arno Press and the New York Times.

Gans, Herbert J.
 1962   The Urban Villagers: Group and Class in the Life
 of Italian-Americans. New York: The Free Press.

Gluckman, Max
 1968   The Utility of the Equilibrium Model in the Study
 of Social Change. American Anthropologist 70:219-237.

Goldhamer, Herbert
1951   Voluntary Associations in the United States.   In
Reader in Urban Sociology. Paul Hatt and Albert Reiss,
eds. New York: Free Press.

Goldkind, Victor
1963   Factors in the Differential Acculturation of
Mexicans in a Michigan City. Unpublished Ph.D.
Dissertation, Michigan State University.

Goldner, Norman
1959   The Mexican in the Northern Urban Area: A
Comparison of Two Generations. Unpublished Ph.D.
Dissertation, University of Minnesota.

Goldstein, Sidney
1958   Patterns of Mobility: 1910-1950: A Method for
Measuring Migration and Occupational Mobility in the
Community. Philadelphia: University of Pennsylvania
Press.

Gollin, Gillian Lindt
1967   Moravians in Two Worlds: A Study of Changing
Communities. New York: Columbia University Press.

Gonzales, Kathleen May
1928   The Mexican Family in San Antonio. Unpublished
M.A. Thesis, University of Texas.

Gordon, C. Wayne, and Nicholas Babchuk
1959   A Typology of Voluntary Associations. American
Sociological Review 24:22-29.

Grant, Madison and Charles Stewart Davison, eds.
1930   The Alien in our Midst or "Selling Our Birthright
for a Mess of Industrial Pottage." New York: The
Galton Publishing Co., Inc.

Grebler, Leo, Joan W. Moore, and Ralph C. Guzman
  1970 The Mexican-American People: The Nation's Second
    Largest Minority. New York: The Free Press.

Green, Vera M.
  1969 Aspects of Interethnic Intergration in Aruba,
    Netherlands Antilles. Unpublished Ph.D. Dissertation,
    University of Arizona.
  1971 Situational Change and Selection vs. Assimilation
    in Understanding Multi-Ethnic Societies. Paper
    presented at the 70th meeting of the American
    Anthropological Association. New York.

Hamer, John J.
  1967 Voluntary Associations as Structures of Change
    Among the Sidamo of Southwestern Ethiopia.
    Anthropological Quarterly 60:73-91.

Hammond, Dorothy
  1972 Associations. Addison-Wesley Modular Publication,
    No. 14. Reading, Mass.: Addison-Wesley Publishing
    Co.

Handelman, Don
  1967 Leadership, Solidarity and Conflict in West
    Indian Immigrant Associations. Human Organization
    26:118-125.

Harary, F. and R.Z. Norman
  1953 Graph Theory as a Mathematical Model in Social
    Science. Ann Arbor: Institute for Social Research.

Hartman, David
  1972 Adaptation to Complexity: The Renaissance of
    Ethnicity. Paper presented at the meeting of the
    Central States Anthropological Society.

Hausknecht, Marray
1962 The Joiners: A Sociological Description of
Voluntary Association Membership in the United States.
New York: The Bedminster Press.

Heath, Dwight B.
1958 Drinking Patterns of the Bolivian Camba. Quarterly
Journal of Studies on Alcohol 19:491-510.

Heller, Celia S.
1966 Mexican American Youth: Forgotten Youth at the
Crossroads. New York: Random House.

Hertzberg, Hazel W.
1971 The Search for an American Indian Identity: Modern
Pan-Indian Movements. Syracuse: Syracuse University
Press.

Hogg, Thomas Clark
1965 Urban Migrants and Associations in Sub-Saharan
Africa. Unpublished Ph.D. Dissertation, University of
Oregon.

Holsti, Ole R.
1969 Content Analysis for the Social Sciences and
Humanities. Reading, Mass.: Addison-Wesley
Publishing Co.

Horton, Paul B., and Chester L. Hunt
1968 Sociology. New York: McGraw-Hill Book Co.

Hubbell, Linda J.
1971 The Network of Compadrazgo Among Middle-Class
Mexican Women. Paper presented at the 70th meeting of
the American Anthropological Association. New York.

Isbell, Billie Jean
  1972 Migrants' Adaptation of Traditional Symbolic
    Systems to the Urban Environment of Lima. Paper
    presented at the 71st annual meeting of the American
    Anthropological Association. Toronto, Canada.

Jackson, J.A.
  1969a Migration-Editorial Introduction. In Migration.
    J.A. Jackson, ed. Cambridge: Cambridge University
    Press.
  1969b Migration. Cambridge: Cambridge University
    Press.

Jacobson, Eugene
  1956 The Growth of Groups in a Voluntary Association.
    Journal of Social Issues 12:18-23.

Kahl, Joseph A.
  1962 Three Types of Mexican Industrial Workers.
    Economic Development and Cultural Change 8:164-169.

Kapferer, Bruce
  1969 Norms and the Manipulation of Relationships in a
    Work Context. In Social Networks in Urban Situations:
    Analyses of Personal Relationships in Central African
    Towns. J. Clyde Mitchell, ed. Manchester: The
    University Press.

Kearney, Michael.
  1970 Drunkenness and Religious Conversion in a Mexican
    Village. Quarterly Journal of Studies on Alcohol
    31:132-152.

Kenny, Michael
  1961 Twentieth Century Spanish Expatriates in Cuba: A
    Sub-culture? Anthropological Quarterly 34:85-93.
  1962 Twentieth Century Spanish Expatriates in Mexico:
    An Urban Sub-Culture. Anthropological Quarterly
    35:169-180.

Keskulla, John
1971 A Methodology for the Analysis of Ethnic
      Differentiation. Paper presented at the 70th meeting
      of the American Anthropological Association. New York.

Kiev, Ari
1968 Curanderismo: Mexican-American Folk Psychiatry.
      New York: The Free Press.

Kurtz, Norman Rudolph
1966 Gatekeepers in the Process of Acculturation.
      Unpublished Ph.D. Dissertation, University of
      Colorado.

Landman, Ruth
1953 Some Aspects of the Acculturation of Mexican
      Immigrants and their Decendants to American Culture.
      Unpublished Ph.D. Dissertation, Yale University.

Lane, J.H., Jr.
1968 Voluntary Associations Among Mexican Americans in
      San Antonio, Texas: Organizational and Leadership
      Characteristics. Unpublished Ph.D. Dissertation,
      University of Texas at Austin.

Leeds, Anthony
1965 Brazilian Careers and Social Structure: A Case
      History and Model. In Contemporary Cultures and
      Societies of Latin America: A Reader in the Social
      Anthropology of Middle and South America and the
      Caribbean. Dwight B. Heath and Richard N. Adams, eds.
      New York: Random House. Pp. 379-404.

Levine, Donald N.
1965 Wax & Gold: Tradition and Innovation in Ethiopian
      Culture. Chicago: University of Chicago Press.

342

Lex, Barbara W. and Stanley A. West
  1970 The Ins and Outs of Urban Research: General
  Comments with Reference to the Mexican-Americans of
  Bethlehem, Pennsylvania. Paper presented at the
  Conference on Anthropological Research in Cities,
  Milwaukee, Wisconsin.

Lin, Paul Ming-Chang
  1963 Voluntary Kinship and Voluntary Association in a
  Mexican-American Community. Unpublished, M.A. Thesis,
  University of Kansas.

Little, Kenneth
  1965 West African Urbanization: A Study of Voluntary
  Associations in Social Change. Cambridge: Cambridge
  University Press.
  1967 Voluntary Associations in Urban Life: A Case
  Study in Differential Adaptation. In Social Organiza-
  tion: Essays presented to Raymond Firth. Maurice
  Freedman, ed. Chicago: Aldine Publishing Co.
  1968 The Migrant and the Urban Community. In
  Urbanism in World Perspective: A Reader. Sylvia Fleis
  Fava, ed. New York: Thomas Y. Crowell Co.
  1971 Some Aspects of African Urbanization South of the
  Sahara. Reading, Mass.: Addison-Wesley Modular
  Publications.

Lopreato, Joseph
  1967 Peasants No More: Social Class and Social Change
  in an Underdeveloped Society. San Francisco:
  Chandler Publishing Co.

Maccoby, Michael
  1967 Love and Authority: A Study of Mexican Villagers.
  In Peasant Society: A Reader. Jack M. Potter, May N.
  Diaz, and George M. Foster, eds. Boston: Little,
  Brown and Co.

Maccoby, Michael and Nancy Modiano
   1969 Cognitive Style in Rural and Urban Mexico. Human
   Development 12:22-33.

Macklin, Barbara Jane
   1963 Structural Stability and Change in a Mexican-
   American Community. Unpublished Ph.D. Dissertation,
   University of Pennsylvania.

Madsen, William
   1964 The Mexican-Americans of South Texas. New York:
   Holt, Rinehart, and Winston.

Madsen, William, and Claudia Madsen
   1969 The Cultural Structure of Mexican Drinking
   Behavior. Quarterly Journal of Studies on Alcohol
   30:701-718.

Mangin, William P.
   1957 Drinking Among Andean Indians. Quarterly Journal
   of Studies on Alcohol 18:55-65.
   1965 The Role of Regional Associations in the Adaptation
   of Rural Migrants to Cities in Peru. In Contemporary
   Cultures and Societies of Latin America. Dwight B.
   Heath, and Richard N. Adams, eds. New York: Random
   House.

Manning, Caroline
   1930 The Immigrant Women and Her Job. Bulletin of the
   Women's Bureau No. 74, United States Department of
   Labor. Washington D.C.: United States Government
   Printing Office.

Martinez, John R.
   1966 Leadership and Politics. In La Raza: Forgotten
   Americans. Julian Samora, ed. Notre Dame: University
   of Notre Dame Press.

Matthiasson, C.W.
  1968 Acculturation of Mexican-Americans in a Midwestern
  City. Unpublished Ph.D. Dissertation, Cornell
  University.

Meillasoux, Claude
  1968 Urbanization of an African Community: Voluntary
  Associations in Bamako. Seattle: University of
  Washington Press.

Mexican Journeys to Bethlehem
  1923 The Literary Digest 77:103-104.

Mexicans in California: Report of Governor C.C. Young's
  Mexican fact-finding committee.
  1930 State Building, San Francisco, Calif.: California
  State Printing Office.

Minnis, Mhyra S.
  1966 The Influence of Social Structure. In The
  Government of Associations: Selections from the
  Behavioral Sciences. William A. Glaser and David L.
  Sills, eds. Totowa, N.J.: The Bedminster Press, Inc.

Minority Life at the Labor Camp
  1963 Term paper, Sociology 101, Lehigh University
  (typewritten, including hand-drawn map).

Mintz, Sidney, and Eric Wolf
  1967 An Analysis of Ritual Co-Parenthood (Compadrazgo).
  In Peasant Society: A Reader. Jack M. Potter, May N.
  Diaz, and George M. Foster, eds. Boston: Little,
  Brown and Co.

Moquin, Wayne
  1971 A Documentary History of the Mexican Americans.
  New York: Praeger Publishers.

Morning Call (Allentown)
"Ballplayer Awed by New 'Power,'" August 13, 1963, n.p.

Morrill, W.T.
1967 Immigrants and Associations: The Ibo in
Twentieth Century Calabar. In Immigrants and
Associations. Lloyd A. Fallers, ed. The Hague:
Mouton.

Morris, Raymond N.
1965 British and American Research on Voluntary
Associations: A Comparison. Sociological Inquiry
35:186-200.

McGinn, Noel F., Ernest Harburg, and Gerald P. Ginsburg
1965 Responses to Interpersonal Conflict by Middle
Class Males in Guadalajara and Michigan. American
Anthropologist 67:1483-1494.

McWilliams, Carey
1941 Mexicans to Michigan. Common Ground 2:5-18.
1949 North from Mexico: The Spanish-Speaking People of
the United States. Philadelphia: J.B. Lippincott Co.

Noble, Charles
1970 Voluntary Associations of the Basukuma of Northern
Mainland Tanzania. Unpublished Ph.D. Dissertation,
Catholic University of America.

Norbeck, Edward
1966 Rural Japan. In The Government of Associations:
Selections from the Behavioral Sciences. William A.
Glaser and David L. Sills, eds. Totowa, N.J.: The
Bedminster Press, Inc.

North, Robert C., Howard E. Koch, and Dina A. Zinnes
1960 The Integrative Functions of Conflict. Conflict
Resolution 4:355-374.

Nova, Julian
    1971   The Mexican-Americans: An Anthology of Basic
        Readings (from the beginning to the present). New York:
        Van Nostrand Reinhold Co.

Officer, James E.
    1964   Sodalities and Systemic Linkage: The Joining
        Habits of Urban Mexican-Americans. Unpublished Ph.D.
        Dissertation, University of Arizona.

Palisi, Bartolomeo J.
    1965   Ethnic Generation and Social Participation.
        Sociological Inquiry 35:219-226.

Parkin, D.J.
    1966   Urban Voluntary Associations as Institutions of
        Adaptation. Man (N.S.) 1:91-94.

Pelto, Pertti J.
    1970   Anthropological Research: The Structure of Inquiry.
        New York: Harper and Row, Publishers.

The People of Bethlehem
    1967   Community Renewal Program, Report No. 2.   Bethlehem,
        Pa.: Bureau of Planning and Development.

Peenock, J. Roland, and John W. Chapman
    1969   Voluntary Associations. New York: Atherton Press.

Porter, Katherine Anne
    1924   Corridos. The Survey 52:157-159.

La Prensa
    1923   San Antonio

Provinzano, James
    1971   Networks and Migration Sets Among Chicano Migrant
           Farm Workers. Paper presented at the 70th meeting of
           the American Anthropological Association, New York.

Richards, Cara E.
    1963-1964 City Taverns. Human Organization 22:260-268.

Rivera, George Jr.
    1970   Recognition of Local-Cosmopolitan Influentials in
           an Urban Mexican American Barrio. In Mexican Americans
           in the United States: A Reader. John H. Burma, ed.
           Cambridge, Mass.: Schenkman Publishing Co., Inc.

Rollwagen, Jack R.
    1969   Rural-Urban Migration and the Maintenance of
           Corporate Identity. Paper presented to the Invitational
           Workshop on Community Responsibilities and School
           Guidance Programs for Mexican-American Youth, Sponsored
           By Texas Technological College.

Romano V., Octavio Ignacio
    1968   The Anthropology and Sociology of the Mexican-
           Americans: The Distortion of Mexican-American History:
           A Review Essay. El Grito 2:13-26.

Rose, Arnold M.
    1954   A Theory of the Functions of Voluntary Associations
           in Contemporary Social Structure. In Theory and Method
           in the Social Sciences. Minneapolis: The University
           of Minneapolis Press. Pp. 50-71.
    1960   The Impact of Aging on Voluntary Associations. In
           Handbook of Social Gerontology: Societal Aspects of
           Aging. Clark Tibbitts, ed. Chicago: University of
           Chicago Press.

Rubel, Arthur Joseph
    1962 Social Life of Urban Mexican-Americans.
    Unpublished Ph.D. Dissertation, University of North
    Carolina.
    1966 Across the Tracks: Mexican-Americans in a Texas
    City. Austin: University of Texas Press.

Rumbos de Mexico
    Vol. 6, No. 16, September, 1960, p. 11; Vol. 7, No. 17,
    September, 1961, p. 23.

San Antonio Light
    1923

Safa, Helen Icken
    n.d. Assimilation vs. Pluralism: Two Models for the
    Integration of Ethnic Groups in the Americas.
    Department of Anthropology, Livingston College, Rutgers
    University.

Samora, Julian
    1953 Minority Leadership in a Bicultural Community.
    Unpublished Ph.D. Dissertation, Washington University.

Samora, Julian, and Richard A. Lamanna
    1967 Mexican-Americans in a Midwest Metropolis: A
    Study of East Chicago. Mexican-American Study Project,
    Advance Report 8, Los Angeles, Division of Research,
    Graduate School of Business Administration.

Sargi, Albert Louis
    1966 Networks of Discord: A Study of the Communication
    System Between Spanish-Speaking Organizations and their
    Community. Unpublished M.A. Thesis, San Francisco
    State College.

Scott, Robin Fitzgerald
    1971 The Mexican-American in the Los Angeles Area, 1920-
    1950: From Acquiescence to Activity. Unpublished Ph.D.
    Dissertation, University of Southern California.

Scott, W. Richard
1969 Field Methods in the Study of Organization. In A Sociological Reader of Complex Organizations. Amitai Etzioni, ed. New York: Holt, Rinehart and Winston, Inc. Pp. 557-576.

Selvin, Hanan C.
1966 Five Studies of the Effects of Leadership Style. In The Government of Associations: Selections from the Behavioral Sciences. William A. Glaser, and David L. Sills, eds. Totawa, N.J.: The Bedminster Press, Inc.

Senior, Clarence
1962 Migration as a Process and Migrant as a Person. The Population Review 6:30-41.

Servin, Manuel P.
1970 The Mexican-Americans: An Awakening Minority. Beverly Hills: Glencoe Press.

Sheldon, Paul
1966 Community Participation and the Emergent Middle Class. In La Raza: Forgotten Americans. Julian Samora, ed. Notre Dame, University of Notre Dame Press.
1970 Mexican American Formal Organizations. In Mexican-Americans in the United States: A Reader. John H. Burma, ed. Cambridge, Mass.: Schenkman Publishing Co., Inc.

Sills, David L.
1959 Voluntary Associations as Instruments and Objects of Change. Human Organization 18:17-21.
1966 Goal Succession in Four Voluntary Associations. In The Government of Associations: Selections from the Behavioral Sciences. William A. Glaser and David L. Sills, eds. Totowa, N.J.: The Bedminster Press, Inc.
1968 Voluntary Associations: Sociological Aspects. In International Encyclopedia of the Social Sciences. D.L. Sills, ed. New York: Macmillan.

Simmons, Merle E.
1957   The Mexican Corrido as a Source of Interpretive
Study of Mexico (1870-1950).   Bloomington, Ind.:
Indiana University Press.

Simmons, Ozzie G.
1968   The Sociocultural Integration of Alcohol Use: A
Peruvian Study.   Quarterly Journal of Studies on
Alcohol 29:152-171.

Soen, Dan, and Patrice DeComarmond
1972   Savings Associations Among the Bamileke:
Traditional and Modern Cooperation in the Southwest
Cameroon.   American Anthropologist 74:1170-1179.

Spinrad, William
1960   Correllates of Trade Union Participation: A
Summary of the Literature.   American Sociological
Review 25:237-244.

Stein, Howard F.
1971   Ethnic Identification vs. Identity as Ethnic:
Americans of Slovak Descent in Urban-Industrial Western
Pennsylvania.   Paper presented at the 70th meeting of
the American Anthropological Association, New York.

Steiner, Stan
1970   La Laza: The Mexican Americans.   New York: Harper
and Row, Publishers.

Stross, Brian
1967   The Mexican Cantina as a Setting for Interaction.
The Kroeber Anthropological Society Papers, No. 37.
Berkeley: Kroeber Anthropological Society.

Sullenger, T. Earl
1924   The Mexican Population of Omaha.   Journal of Applied
Sociology 8:289-293.

Tannenbaum, Arnold S.
  1961 Control and Effectiveness in a Voluntary
  Organization. American Journal of Sociology
  67:33-46.

Taylor, Paul S.
  1931a Mexican Labor in the United States: Imperial
  Valley, Vol. I. University of California Publications
  in Economics VI, No. 1. Berkeley, Calif.: University
  of California Press.
  1931b Mexican Labor in the United States: Bethlehem,
  Pennsylvania. University of California Publications
  in Economics, VII, No. 1. Berkeley, Calif.:
  University of California Press.
  1932 Mexican Labor in the United States: Chicago and
  the Calumet Region. University of California
  Publication in Economics, VII, No. 2. Berkeley:
  University of California Press.
  1933 A Spanish-Mexican Peasant Community: Arandas in
  Jalisco, Mexico. Ibero-Americana, No. 4. Berkeley,
  Calif.: University of California Press.
  1934 An Mexican-American Frontier. Chapel Hill:
  University of North Carolina Press.

Treudley, Mary
  1966 The Transformation of Peasants into Citizens. In
  The Government of Associations: Selections from the
  Behavioral Sciences. William A. Glaser and David L.
  Sills, eds. Totowa, N.J.: The Bedminster Press, Inc.

Tsouderos, John E.
  1953 The Formalization Process of the Social Structure
  in Voluntary Associations. Unpublished Ph.D.
  Dissertation, University of Minnesota.
  1955 Organizational Change in Terms of a Series of
  Selected Variables. American Sociological Review
  20:206-210.

Tumin, Melvin
  1957 Some Unapplauded Consequences of Social Mobility
    in Mass Society. Social Forces 36:32-37.

Vaca, Nick C.
  1970 The Mexican-American in the Social Sciences, 1912-
    1970; Part II: 1936-1970. El Grito 4:17-51.

Vadasz, Thomas
  1967 The South Bethlehem Strike of 1910. Unpublished
    M.S.
  n.d. Untitled unpublished M.S.

Vogt, Evon Z.
  1970 The Zinacantecos of Mexico: A Modern Maya Way of
    Life. New York: Holt, Rinehart and Winston.

Wallace, Anthony F.C.
  1970 Culture and Personality. 2nd ed. New York:
    Random House.

Wallerstein, Immanuel M.
  1964 The Road to Independence: Ghana and the Ivory
    Coast. Paris: Mouton & Co.
  1966 Voluntary Associations. In Political Arties and
    National Integration in Tropical Africa. James S.
    Coleman and Carl G. Rosenberg, Jr., eds. Berkeley:
    University of California Press.

Warner, W. Lloyd
  1953 American Life: Dream and Reality. Chicago:
    University of Chicago Press.

Warriner, Charles K., and Jane Emory Prather
  1965 Four Types of Voluntary Associations. Sociological
    Inquiry 35:138-148.

Watson, James B., and Julian Samora
  1954 Subordinate Leadership in a Bicultural Community:
    An Analysis. American Sociological Review 19:413-421.

Wheeldon, P.D.
    1969 The Operation of Voluntary Associations and Personal
    Networks in the Political Processes of an Inter-
    Ethnic Community. In Social Networks in Urban Situa-
    tions: Analyses of Personal Relationships in Central
    African Towns. J. Clyde Mitchell, ed. Manchester:
    Manchester University Press.

Whitten, Norman E. Jr.
    1970 Network Analysis and Processes of Adaptation Among
    Ecuadorian and Nova Scotian Negroes. In Marginal
    Natives: Anthropologists at Work. Morris Freilich,
    ed. New York: Harper and Row, Publishers.

Yates, W. Ross
    1963 History of the Lehigh Valley Region. Joint
    Planning Commission, Lehigh and Northampton Counties.

BIOGRAPHICAL DATA

Name: Stanley A. West

Date and Place of Birth: May 21, 1943
                          Bath, New York

Elementary School: Franklin Academy and Prattsburg
                    Central School
                    Prattsburg, New York
                    Graduated 1955

High School: Franklin Academy and
              Prattsburg Central School
              Prattsburg, New York
              Graduated 1961

College: Syracuse University
          Syracuse, New York
          B. S. 1965

Graduate Work: Syracuse University
                Syracuse, New York

THE CHICANO HERITAGE

An Arno Press Collection

Adams, Emma H. **To and Fro in Southern California.** 1887

Anderson, Henry P. **The Bracero Program in California.** 1961

Aviña, Rose Hollenbaugh. **Spanish and Mexican Land Grants in California.** 1976

Barker, Ruth Laughlin. **Caballeros.** 1932

Bell, Horace. **On the Old West Coast.** 1930

Biberman, Herbert. **Salt of the Earth.** 1965

Casteñeda, Carlos E., trans. **The Mexican Side of the Texas Revolution (1836).** 1928

Casteñeda, Carlos E. **Our Catholic Heritage in Texas, 1519-1936.** Seven volumes. 1936-1958

Colton, Walter. **Three Years in California.** 1850

Cooke, Philip St. George. **The Conquest of New Mexico and California.** 1878

Cue Canovas, Agustin. **Los Estados Unidos Y El Mexico Olvidado.** 1970

Curtin, L. S. M. **Healing Herbs of the Upper Rio Grande.** 1947

Fergusson, Harvey. **The Blood of the Conquerors.** 1921

Fernandez, Jose. **Cuarenta Años de Legislador:** Biografia del Senador Casimiro Barela. 1911

Francis, Jessie Davies. **An Economic and Social History of Mexican California** (1822-1846). Volume I: Chiefly Economic. Two vols. in one. 1976

Getty, Harry T. **Interethnic Relationships in the Community of Tucson.** 1976

Guzman, Ralph C. **The Political Socialization of the Mexican American People.** 1976

Harding, George L. **Don Agustin V. Zamorano.** 1934

Hayes, Benjamin. **Pioneer Notes from the Diaries of Judge Benjamin Hayes, 1849-1875.** 1929

Herrick, Robert. **Waste.** 1924

Jamieson, Stuart. **Labor Unionism in American Agriculture.** 1945

Landolt, Robert Garland. **The Mexican-American Workers of San Antonio, Texas.** 1976

Lane, Jr., John Hart. **Voluntary Associations Among Mexican Americans in San Antonio, Texas.** 1976

Livermore, Abiel Abbot. **The War with Mexico Reviewed.** 1850

Loyola, Mary. **The American Occupation of New Mexico, 1821-1852.** 1939

Macklin, Barbara June. **Structural Stability and Culture Change in a Mexican-American Community.** 1976

McWilliams, Carey. **Ill Fares the Land:** Migrants and Migratory Labor in the United States. 1942

Murray, Winifred. **A Socio-Cultural Study of 118 Mexican Families Living in a Low-Rent Public Housing Project in San Antonio, Texas.** 1954

Niggli, Josephina. **Mexican Folk Plays.** 1938

Parigi, Sam Frank. **A Case Study of Latin American Unionization in Austin, Texas.** 1976

Poldervaart, Arie W. **Black-Robed Justice.** 1948

Rayburn, John C. and Virginia Kemp Rayburn, eds. **Century of Conflict, 1821-1913.** Incidents in the Lives of William Neale and William A. Neale, Early Settlers in South Texas. 1966

Read, Benjamin. **Illustrated History of New Mexico.** 1912

Rodriguez, Jr., Eugene. **Henry B. Gonzalez.** 1976

Sanchez, Nellie Van de Grift. **Spanish and Indian Place Names of California.** 1930

Sanchez, Nellie Van de Grift. **Spanish Arcadia.** 1929

Shulman, Irving. **The Square Trap.** 1953

Tireman, L. S. **Teaching Spanish-Speaking Children.** 1948

Tireman, L. S. and Mary Watson. **A Community School in a Spanish-Speaking Village.** 1948

Twitchell, Ralph Emerson. **The History of the Military Occupation of the Territory of New Mexico.** 1909

Twitchell, Ralph Emerson. **The Spanish Archives of New Mexico.** Two vols. 1914

U. S. House of Representatives. **California and New Mexico:** Message from the President of the United States, January 21, 1850. 1850

Valdes y Tapia, Daniel. **Hispanos and American Politics.** 1976

West, Stanley A. **The Mexican Aztec Society.** 1976

Woods, Frances Jerome. **Mexican Ethnic Leadership in San Antonio, Texas.** 1949

3 0511 00569 1159